purity

Other Crossway books by
Lydia Brownback:

Trust
Contentment
Joy

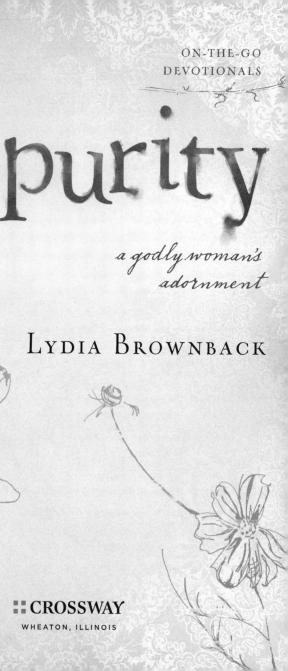

purity

*a godly woman's
adornment*

LYDIA BROWNBACK

∷ **CROSSWAY**
WHEATON, ILLINOIS

Library of Congress Cataloging-in-Publication Data
Brownback, Lydia, 1963–
   Purity: a godly woman's adornment / Lydia Brownback.
      p. cm. — (On-the-go devotionals)
   ISBN 978-1-4335-1298-8 (tpb)
   1. Christian women—Prayers and devotions. 2. Purity (Ethics)—Prayers and devotions. I. Title. II. Series.
BV4844.B77   2010
242'.643—dc22   2009040912

With gratitude to God

for the friendship of

Elyse Fitzpatrick, Sherah Grose,

Ruthie Howard, Leslie Lindner,

and Laurie Lynch

Contents

Pure in Body

Sexual Purity

Pure Love

Part One

A Pure Heart

*W*e don't hear the word *purity* much today except in descriptions of cleaning agents and snow-covered landscapes. We do hear the word spoken more frequently in the Christian community, but usually only as it applies to sexual purity. We have lost sight of all it means to be pure as God intended. So what does it mean? Purity is much more than moral behavior. Purity is first and foremost a matter of the heart. To be pure is to be single-minded. It is to have a single goal, a single focus, and a single purpose for ourselves and our lives. That is biblical purity, and from it springs moral behavior—the good we do with our bodies. At its core, purity is having a heart for the Lord that isn't watered down or polluted by lesser things.

The apostle James wrote, "Cleanse your hands, you sinners; and purify your hearts, you double-minded." According to James, a double-minded woman spends her passion going after what this world offers. In contrast, Jesus describes a very different sort of passion: "You shall love the Lord your God with all your heart, and with all your soul, and with all your mind. This is the great and first commandment" (Matt. 22:37–38). Elsewhere Jesus attaches a promise to purity: "Blessed are the pure in heart, for they shall see God" (Matt.

5:8). To see God is to know the joy of living in close relationship with him. To see him is also to enjoy Spirit-filled, biblically guided direction and guidance for all of life. A woman who is pure in this way realizes an ever-increasing ability to rightly apply God's Word to the little day-to-day things.

Putting Christ first is the essence of purity. That is why Jesus' words in the beatitude, "Blessed are the pure in heart, for they shall see God," are the starting point for any woman who is serious about being pure. But the beatitude is not only our starting point; it is also the place to end. Jesus' words form the basis for the kind of purity that will endure for a lifetime. Viewing purity from a biblical perspective takes our understanding of what it means to be pure beyond mere outward conduct to a whole new level—a deeper level. And if we approach purity as Jesus describes it, we will discover that our battle to be pure in body, as well as in mind and spirit, comes much more easily.

We women struggle, often with little success, to master particular sins—outward displays of impurity. Perhaps that's because we have been trying to clean up our act while failing to see the impurity in our heart. What are we to do? We can't clean our own heart. Besides, the extent of its dirt and sin is beyond our comprehension. A heart is made pure as Christ washes and cleans it. I once heard someone pray, "Lord, wash my heart." That's a good prayer. But becoming pure in heart doesn't end with prayer. It comes as we lean on the purity of Christ, on his perfect work for us. It comes as we lean on grace. It comes as we acknowledge our utter inability to become pure women and our need for Christ to make us clean and to purify us through and through. Putting Christ first takes care of everything else.

A Pure Woman Is Clear-sighted

Blessed are the pure in heart, for they shall see God.

MATTHEW 5:8

*J*esus chose to begin his great sermon, the Sermon on the Mount, with a list of blessings. There are nine, to be exact, and each blessing is given to a specific sort of person. All too often we are quick to pass over this initial part of the sermon, which is called the Beatitudes. We want to get on to the practical parts of Jesus' teaching, where he talks about things like marriage and money and dealing with difficult emotions (Matthew 5–7). Perhaps we are quick to skim over the Beatitudes because we don't quite understand exactly what Jesus was getting at. The sixth beatitude, "Blessed are the pure in heart, for they shall see God," is a case in point. What does it mean to be pure in heart? And how can we actually *see* God?

When we think of purity, sexual purity is usually the first thing that comes to mind. But that's not Jesus' emphasis here in his sermon. He emphasizes heart purity. Not for a minute is Jesus diminishing the importance of sexual purity and all we do with our bodies, but he emphasizes heart purity because it is the root from which all other purity springs. If we are pure in heart, we will be pure in body too. A pure heart is an undivided heart, one with a single purpose. A pure heart is one so set on God that it isn't watered down by lesser things. Does that describe your heart? It does if your driving passion in life is to know God and live in close fellowship with him.

To the pure in heart Jesus promised the blessing of sight. But he wasn't talking about a visual image; he was talking about comprehension. The more focused on God we are, the more of him we will know; and the better we know him, the more blessed we will be, because we will see that the most awesome, powerful being in the universe is also kind, loving, and relational.

The purer we are, the more we will see. But we miss out on the blessing of sight because we don't have pure hearts. Our hearts are divided. We want God, but we also want the comforts and pleasures that the world offers. The things of this life will ultimately never satisfy us because we were designed to find real fulfillment in God alone. A woman who is pure in heart is able to enjoy the good things God puts in her life, but those things don't hold her heart. God alone has that place because her view of his goodness, love, and wonder is much less cluttered up with the junk of the world.

If we are missing out on this blessedness, it doesn't have to be that way. We don't have to spend our lives running after lesser and short-lived ways of feeling satisfied with life. If this weren't true, Jesus wouldn't have given the beatitude. But he did give it, and he holds it out to us today. Do we really want it? That's the question.

A Pure Woman Has One Desire

Whom have I in heaven but you?
And there is nothing on earth that I desire besides you.

PSALM 73:25

*T*here is nothing on earth that I desire besides you"—with these words the psalmist gives us the ultimate definition of a pure heart. Can you echo his words? Is there truly nothing we desire besides God? Perhaps you want to be like this, but you just aren't there yet, and you aren't sure how to get there. Maybe you have tasted it, but you can't seem to hang on to it. Life's pressures mount and close in around you, and the desire for relief crowds out the desire for God himself.

God wants us to know what it's like to desire nothing but him. That's why he allows us to find such little lasting satisfaction with the world's toys and joys. We get something we've always wanted, or a dream comes true, yet it quickly becomes just part of life's routine. So what do we do? We set out to lay hold of some new earthbound pleasure. We don't stop to consider that our inability to find lasting happiness in earthly blessings and personal dreams is because God designed us for something else. Our dissatisfaction is his way of wooing us to find our all in him.

We don't have to remain dissatisfied. We can know God the

way he wants to be known. The way to get there is the same way the psalmist Asaph got there, and Psalm 73 recounts his journey. At one point, he was just like most of us at times—dissatisfied with life. In fact, he was more than simply dissatisfied; he was resentful. He looked around and saw that people who make no effort to follow God seem to get more from this life than the faithful. It made no sense to him, and Asaph was resentful—and jealous. "As for me, my feet had almost stumbled, my steps had nearly slipped. For I was envious of the arrogant when I saw the prosperity of the wicked" (vv. 2–3).

Asaph goes on verse after verse recounting the many outward blessings that seem to come to worldly people. We can see from his detailed account that he'd spent a lot of time comparing his life to theirs, and he felt that his life came up short. All his comparing was nothing more than grumbling, and it warped his view of God, as complaining always does. Grumbling against what God ordains in our lives makes him seem small in our eyes, and, of course, when God seems small to us, we aren't going to desire him very much. That's where Asaph had allowed himself to go, and that left him focused squarely on the pleasures, the wealth, and the seeming security enjoyed by those who pour their energies into maximizing what they can from this life. "Behold, these are the wicked; always at ease, they increase in riches" (v. 12). Asaph felt gypped, and his obsession shaped his thinking: "All in vain have I kept my heart clean and washed my hands in innocence" (v. 13).

Do you ever feel that way? Are there times when you question whether Christian discipleship is worth it? Jesus said that those who follow him may have to forego much of what this world has to offer. He also said that the benefits of following him ultimately outweigh the cost, but when the going gets rough, we begin to have second thoughts. Oh, most of us don't turn our backs on Jesus and refuse to walk with him any longer; what we do instead is try to have it both ways. We get up in the morning and read our Bible and practice outward obedience, but we are pouring as much if not more of our time and energy into comfort, pleasure, success, and being loved by people. When it comes right down to it, we want God, but we want what everyone else has too.

What turned the psalmist around? How did he go from an envious grumbler to a pure-hearted worshiper? The turning point came for Asaph when he stopped looking around him and began to look up. He went into "the sanctuary of God" (v. 17) and from there he was able to see the reality of things. Looking at God brings everything else into proper focus. When we look at things through the lens of our personal perspective, everything we see is going to be warped. But the only way to know that our perspective is misshapen is by looking at everything through the lens of Scripture. Asaph found it in the sanctuary; we find it in God's Word. Like Asaph, if we look through the right lens we will be able to see that those who have God have everything, and those who do not have God really have nothing.

We get pure hearts by looking away from the world and up to God, and we see him in Scripture. As we do that, we will find what Asaph found:

> When my soul was embittered,
>   when I was pricked in heart,
> I was brutish and ignorant;
>   I was like a beast before you.
> Nevertheless, I am continually with you;
>   you hold my right hand.

You guide me with your counsel,
    and afterward you will receive me to glory.
Whom have I in heaven but you?
    And there is nothing on earth that I desire besides you.
My flesh and my heart may fail,
    but God is the strength of my heart and my portion forever. (vv. 21–26)

A Pure Woman Is Single-minded

Draw near to God, and he will draw near to you.
Cleanse your hands, you sinners, and purify your hearts,
you double-minded.

JAMES 4:8

There is a strong link between our hearts and our minds. In fact, Scripture doesn't really differentiate between the two. What we think *is* our heart. Therefore, a double-minded woman is one with a divided heart, and a divided heart isn't a pure heart. James's point is that a double-minded woman is literally two-minded; she is divided between two ways of thinking, and, as a result, she is ruled by competing options.

The problem is that we are all double-minded. We want God *and* a husband, God *and* a better house, or God *and* a more fulfilling job. The *and* is what makes us double-minded. We well know that many of the things we want are good things. God has designed us to enjoy many of them, and he delights to give them to us. So it's not the actual wanting that makes us divided. It's the fact that we believe we must have them in order to be happy. If we believe there is something—anything—essential for our well-being besides God, we are double-minded.

This seems to fly in the face of reason, doesn't it? After

all, certain things are necessary for our well-being, such as food, shelter, fellowship, and health. We must have some things in order to live, and we must pursue them in order to survive. But James's point is that even survival isn't the most important thing in life. If we live with an eternal perspective, earthly happiness and even survival won't own us.

The apostle Paul said, "For to me to live is Christ, and to die is gain. . . . Yet which I shall choose I cannot tell. I am hard pressed between the two. My desire is to depart and be with Christ, for that is far better" (Phil. 1:21–23). Earthly happiness—and even survival—were low on Paul's priority list. Unlike Paul, when we talk wishfully about departing this life it's usually because we are depressed. Depressed people don't care about living. But Paul's desire didn't spring from depression. In fact, Paul was one of the happiest people who ever lived. We know this because in that same epistle he also wrote, "I have learned in whatever situation I am to be content" (4:11), and "Rejoice in the Lord always; again I will say, Rejoice" (4:4). He even survival as expendable because he knew firsthand—perhaps more than anyone else ever has—what Jesus promised: "Blessed are the pure in heart, for they shall see God" (Matt. 5:8). Paul shows us what that means: rejoicing and desiring to be with God so much that we are happy to live or die. Who wouldn't want that?

According to James, the way to a pure heart, the way to know what Paul knew, comes as a result of changing our thinking. We are to become single-minded rather than allowing ourselves to remain double-minded. James is also clear that we are not to be passive in the process; it is something *we* are told to do. There is no "let go and let God" to be found here. It is true that we cannot actually change ourselves; God changes us. He does so as we set our minds on him and . ways. But we won't set ourselves in this direction unless we believe that what we give up in this process is worth the cost. We can't have it both ways, but we are always going to try unless we are convinced that living for Christ is well worth whatever lesser things we lose along the way.

Single-mindedness is the path to a pure heart, which is why Paul wrote, "Do not conform any longer to the pattern of this world, but be transformed by the renewing of your mind. Then you will be able to test and approve what God's will is—his good, pleasing and perfect will" (Rom. 12:2 NIV). Good and acceptable and perfect—to whom? "Not to God, of course," writes James Boice. "That is obvious. Besides, we do not have to prove that God is pleased by his own will, nor could we." Dr. Boice adds:

> When Paul encourages us to prove that God's will is a pleasing will, he obviously means pleasing to us. That is, if we determine to walk in God's way, refusing to be conformed to the world and being transformed instead by the renewing of our minds, we will not have to fear that at the end of our lives we will look back and be dissatisfied or bitter, judging our lives to have been an utter waste. On the contrary, we will look back and conclude that our lives were well lived and be satisfied with them.[1]

---

[1] James Boice, *Romans, Vol. 4: The New Humanity* (Grand Rapids, MI: Baker, 1995), 1558–9.

merciful you show yourself merciful;
meless man you show yourself blameless;
with the purified you show yourself pure;
and with the crooked you make yourself seem tortuous.

Psalm 18:25-26

Do you yearn to be in God's company, or is meeting with him in his Word and in prayer an exercise you have to make yourself do? Perhaps for you it ebbs and flows. At times you are eager to learn all you can about God and to slip off alone with your Bible for an hour of quiet and prayer, but at other times Bible reading feels like a chore, and when you prepare for worship you find yourself thinking more about the people you'll see at church than about meeting with God. Why does this happen? What makes God appealing to us sometimes but not so much at other times? After all, he doesn't change (Heb. 13:8).

Although God doesn't change, our perception of him does. Sometimes we perceive him as a welcoming father but at other times as an unfriendly taskmaster. Our desire for God will always be determined by our perception of God, and what determines our perception of him is the state of our heart. The psalmist makes the connection abundantly clear.

If we find God and his Word confusing or frustrating, it's because something in our heart is resistant to him and his truth. He puts his finger on something in our life—a particular sin or bad habit or worldly pattern of living—and we don't like the intrusion. We want to keep doing what we have been doing. If we persist in it, then over time our resistance to God's way will warp our view of God himself. We follow the same pattern in all our relationships. If a teenager is issued a curfew that she thinks is unfair, she is going to resent her parents and think they are mean. This sort of view is what the psalmist meant when he wrote, "With the crooked you make yourself seem tortuous." Conversely, if the teen trusts her parents' judgment, that they are indeed setting limits for her safety and long-term blessing, then her view of them won't be shaped by the restriction of the curfew.

We see in the psalmist's words more of what Jesus meant when he said that the pure in heart will see God. A pure-hearted woman has a more accurate assessment of God's ways with her and of the things he allows into her life. The more committed we are in our devotion to the Lord, the clearer we will see him, and the clearest views of God are the ones that reveal to us his kindness, care, affection, interest, power, humility, and majesty.

How do you see God today? Do you long to pour out your heart to him, trustful that he is eager to hear you and to reveal himself to you through his Word? Or do you find yourself itching to get on with the day and out with the crowds? Someone once said, "God is always who you know him to be when you are closest to him." The fact remains that no matter how you perceive God today, he is still your Father if you trust in Christ.

A Pure Woman Treasures God's Word

How can a young man keep his way pure?
By guarding it according to your word.
With my whole heart I seek you;
let me not wander from your commandments!

PSALM 119:9–10

*L*ove at first sight—has this ever happened to you? Probably not, because it is virtually impossible to love someone you don't really know. "Love at first sight" or "You had me at 'hello'" is really about the infatuation that occurs when feelings, thoughts, and hormones have a head-on collision. Real love is always based on knowledge, and such knowledge comes from the intimacy produced through shared confidences and experiences. The same holds true in our relationship with God. We won't love him purely if we don't know him, and the only way we will know him is by means of his Word.

That is why we find a strong link between purity and a passion for God in Psalm 119. This psalm is an acrostic poem written in praise of Scripture. According to the psalmist, to be pure is to be wholehearted; it is to have our heart set on just one thing—the pursuit of God and his ways. But we will never develop a heart like that by ourselves. The Holy Spirit uses Scripture to transform us—our interests, our hopes, our desires—so that we increasingly love what he loves and hate what he hates. We will never love God purely—whole-heartedly—apart from immersing ourselves in God's Word because it is only in Scripture that we learn what God is like. To know him is to love him, and we always desire more of what we love most.

"I hate the double-minded, but I love your law. Give me understanding, that I may keep your law and observe it with my whole heart," the psalmist prays (vv. 13, 34). Perhaps this is the passage that the apostle James was thinking of when he wrote, "Cleanse your hands, you sinners, and purify your hearts, you double-minded" (James 4:8). James and the psalmist make clear that purity can characterize only those who have set themselves in a single direction, and we will set ourselves in that direction only if we love what we are pursuing.

Again, the reason we are so often defeated in our battle for purity is that we are torn in two directions. We love God and his ways, but we love other things equally, if not more, and because of that we seek God for what he will give us rather than just for himself.

The psalmist tells us that purity comes by guarding our hearts according to the Word, but guarding our hearts in this way involves much more than simply mining God's Word for a list of do's and don'ts. It is really about the discovery of the character of the One who gave that Word. The Bible is God's autobiography. It is the way we get to know him intimately, the sort of knowing that fosters deep love and devotion.

A Pure Woman Abides in Christ

Who can say, "I have made my heart pure;
I am clean from my sin"?

PROVERBS 20:9

Saturday mornings are the times I set apart for writing. There are few things I enjoy more than curling up in the cozy chair that overlooks my backyard, laptop open, writing the morning away. But as I began work on this devotional, my delightful routine didn't work that way. I'd sit down ready to write, but on several consecutive Saturdays I felt stuck. The writing just wouldn't flow. So after spinning my wheels for an hour or two, I'd pack it in and go do something else, hoping for greater inspiration the following week. But as the publisher's deadline loomed, I had to persevere, writing even when it didn't flow easily. God eventually answered my prayers for help, but not in the way I'd expected. Rather than simply unclogging the writer's block, he showed me something in my heart that was causing it: I was trying to write about a topic in which I know myself to be an utter failure. How could I write a devotional about purity when I know myself to be far from it? The essence of purity is wholeheartedness—being singularly devoted to God in thought, word, and deed—and I know that I fall far short.

As I wrestled with this, I was reminded that God doesn't call us to do something because we are up to the task. He calls us because he is extending to us the privilege of being used by him. The apostle Paul was very sure of his high calling as an apostle, yet at the same time he saw himself as the chief of sinners. If he were to have backed away from his calling on the grounds of personal inadequacy, it would have been due to pride, not humility. If God calls us to a task, he will equip us for it, because it is he who is working through us to that end. The best preachers are those who know they are preaching to themselves as well as to their congregations; in fact, they know that the Holy Spirit is actually the one doing the preaching. They are just the mouthpiece. That was the key to unlocking my writer's block.

It is also the key to unlocking what blocks our pursuit of purity. We know our hearts, and we have to admit that we aren't pure. Our hearts desire far more than just God; we toy with impure fantasies about one thing or another, and we overindulge our appetites and desires—even good ones—on a regular basis. After repeated failures, our growth in the Christian life seems stuck in neutral, and we are tempted just to give up growing altogether. But recognizing our inadequacy is actually the best place to find ourselves, because growth in purity can begin only when we recognize that we can't become pure by ourselves. As the proverb makes plain, we are not pure, and no matter how hard we try to be, we just can't get there. Just as soon as we find ourselves doing better in one area, we fall flat in another. The battle never ceases, and discouragement sets in. But discouragement about our personal abilities is not necessarily bad, and in some cases it is very good. Recognizing our inability to purify our hearts is one of those cases, because only then will we go where real change can occur—to Christ.

Jesus never sinned. He was completely pure in thought, word, and deed. And not only did he die for us; he also lived for us. Jesus "did" purity for us. That means although we aren't pure, God considers us pure because we are in Christ. The victory is sure, because it has already been won for us. That's why we can pursue purity with hope and confidence despite our many failures. That's why we can press on in our labors for God's kingdom, knowing, as we do, our utter inadequacy. "But we have this treasure in jars of clay, to show that the surpassing power belongs to God and not to us" (2 Cor. 4:7).

The Devil is a liar who tells us that we might as well give up the fight for purity. He will do anything he can to sabotage our joy and usefulness. Attempting to improve ourselves just isn't effective counter strategy. Clinging to Christ is the only way.

A Pure Woman Loves the Lord

All the ways of a man are pure in his own eyes,
but the LORD weighs the spirit.

PROVERBS 16:2

A home in which Christ is central is a haven of blessing for those who live there. Among God's greatest gifts are shared prayer around the dinner table, family devotions, and household rules that spring from biblical principles. Yet there is a hidden danger that can accompany that blessing. Children who grow up in solid Christian homes may master the rules but fail to recognize that conformity and obeying Christian practices are not necessarily indicators of true faith.

True faith is never family tradition. We must make sure our faith is not our parents' faith or our spouse's or our pastor's. It's easy to trick ourselves about this, and often the only way we really know that our faith is really *ours* is when we grow up and leave home or when our leader is taken from us in one way or another. The purity of our heart will be revealed only when it is tested, and it is not likely to be tested when someone else makes the majority of our decisions for us.

Whether or not we are surrounded by strong Christian

leadership, we are susceptible to self-deception. "The heart is deceitful above all things, and desperately sick; who can understand it?" (Jer. 17:9). Refraining from physical intimacy until marriage, avoiding drunkenness, and paying our bills on time are certainly obedience to God, but those things can all be done with no love in our heart for him. Love for God is the essence of purity. We cannot be pure without love, but we can perform "clean" actions without love. It is easy to blur the distinction and not even know it.

Growing love in a relationship involves an investment of both time and emotional sacrifice. Good relationships require persevering through the rough patches and laboring to know another. This is true of our human relationships, and it is true of our relationship with God. There are times when he seems hard to understand or obey, and there are times when our sin and selfishness interfere with the enjoyment of our communion with Christ. But if we are *in* Christ, we are going to persevere against the obstacles and setbacks.

Nevertheless, when we hit the rough patches in our Christian walk, it is often easier to simply clean up our act and offer that to God instead of investing what it takes to really know him. Cleaning up is often the easiest thing to offer to God because it costs us so little in comparison to what we know he really wants—our *selves*. It's much easier to shut out sinful fantasies than to ask God to conform us to Christ at any cost. It's must easier to break a questionable habit than to embrace with joy an unchangeable difficulty. It is also easier to simply clean up, because the personal pay—off works to our benefit saying no to sin and overindulgence conduces to our profit. God designed it that way. But he never did so in order that we could enjoy life apart from a real relationship with him. It's just the opposite.

Outward purity will never please God if that purity isn't motivated by love for him. If you have been playing by the rules, yet God seems far from you, stop and consider the relationship. Are you offering him your whole heart or just clean hands?

A Pure Woman Is Discerning

Even a child makes himself known by his acts,
by whether his conduct is pure and upright.

*O*nly God knows what's really in our hearts, but we get clues about what's in there, and those clues are revealed in our behavior. Proverbs 20:11 offers us a purity barometer, a test we can apply to help us grow in godliness and protect ourselves in it. We need this because we are self-deceived women. None of us has an accurate grasp of who we really are. When we see someone get so entangled in a circumstance that she becomes confused about what to do, we often say, "She can't see the forest through the trees." Well, much of the time, that is true of us spiritually. We cannot see the forest of our hearts because the trees of our thoughts, impressions, and feelings crowd in upon us and skew our perspective. But God shows us in this verse from Proverbs a way to clear our vision: we can consider our actions. Our conduct is always a key to our hearts.

We may think we trust God, but our efforts to anxiously control the details of our lives and the lives of those around us show us that we really don't. We may feel the emotion of love for our spouse, but our daily outbursts of anger and irritation reveal something else. We may say we aren't greedy for money or possessions, but our credit card debt shows otherwise. Actions speak louder than words—or feelings—and they reveal what we really believe. A pure heart grows from a willingness to take a good, hard look at our actions and then humbly allow what we see to teach us about ourselves. Do you want accurate self-awareness? Evaluating your actions is a good way to get it.

We can also apply the barometer to the actions of others as we seek to be discerning about associations that might compromise our purity. As Jesus prepared to send out the apostles, he warned them, "Behold, I am sending you out as sheep in the midst of wolves, so be wise as serpents and innocent as doves" (Matt. 10:16). We aren't to pass judgment on others, certainly, and that is where our sinful tendencies can take us when we seek to be discerning about others. "Judge not, that you be not judged" (Matt. 7:1), Jesus said. But the fact remains that we are called to be discerning. Motive is the difference between judging and discerning. If we examine the actions of another and find ourselves feeling superior as a result, we can be quite sure that we are judging. However, if we weigh someone's actions as a means to help her or as a means to guard our own hearts against impurity, then likely we are being discerning.

Applying the behavior barometer is especially helpful in the context of romance. We are at no greater risk for self-deception than when romantic feelings have captured us; few things are as powerful as when two people desire exclusive intimacy with one another. At such times our ability to be objective and discerning is blunted. The man you or I feel passionately about may attend church each week, but what he does in his free time is perhaps a more accurate measure of his heart. He may have all his theological t's crossed, but does he demonstrate love for God in sacrificial service for others?

That being said, the first place to apply the test is to our own actions, not those of another. Will we do this today? If so, we are going to find impurity. As soon as we recognize it, the thing to do is take it straight to the cross. There we will find that Christ has already paid for it. He isn't waiting to condemn us; he is waiting to free us.

A Pure Woman Esteems Christ

*I feel a divine jealousy for you, since I betrothed you
to one husband, to present you as a pure virgin to Christ.
But I am afraid that as the serpent deceived Eve
by his cunning, your thoughts will be led astray from a
sincere and pure devotion to Christ. For if someone comes
and proclaims another Jesus than the one we proclaimed,
or if you receive a different spirit from the one
you received, or if you accept a different gospel from the one
you accepted, you put up with it readily enough.*

2 Corinthians 11:2–4

*W*hat do the apostle Paul and Neil Clark Warren have in
common? The business of matchmaking. Warren uses his
online dating service, eHarmony, to bring couples together,
but Paul matched souls to Christ. That's how Paul presents
himself here, and, in fact, his entire ministry was largely built
around matchmaking. Nothing delighted Paul more than
to lead souls into an exclusive love relationship with Jesus
Christ. Unlike Warren, the apostle Paul was emotionally
involved in each of his matches. He was so connected to every
one that he felt "divine jealousy" when anything threatened
to harm them. In his letter to the Corinthians, Paul was afraid

that false teachers were coming into the church at Corinth and threatening to break up his matches, so he wrote to warn them about the danger.

We, too, have been matched up with Christ, and as a result we belong to him in an exclusive love relationship. But just as with the Corinthians whom Paul was so concerned about, our hearts can be deceived and led astray from this exclusive relationship, one that is supposed to be characterized by pure devotion. How can this happen? Paul shows us, and again we find our minds, or hearts, at the center of the problem. We are led astray through our thoughts.

Apparently this was already happening to the believers in Corinth. People had come into their fellowship and were twisting the truth about Christ and God's kingdom, and Paul accused the Corinthians of tolerating it. "You put up with it readily enough," he said.

What false teaching threatens our sincere and pure devotion to Christ? What do we put up with readily enough? Perhaps today more than anything else, we allow the purity of the true gospel to be diluted by the false gospel of self-esteem. Self-esteem sounds good, but it is antithetical to God's gospel. Christ didn't die to improve our self-esteem; he died to give us his. He didn't come to build up our self-worth; he came to knock it down. Jesus said, "If anyone would come after me, let him deny himself and take up his cross daily and follow me" (Luke 9:24); and Paul wrote, "Do nothing from rivalry or conceit, but in humility count others more significant than yourselves" (Phil. 2:3). We have been deceived by the false teaching of self-esteem because, like most effective deceptions, there is a kernel of truth in it. We do have intrinsic worth because we are made in the image of God. But it is his image in us that gives us our value.

I heard a contemporary Christian song recently in which the singer poured out her gratitude for Christ's death on the cross, but her lyrics reflected a wrong understanding of why Christ died: "What a price I was worth!" Christ didn't go to the cross because she—or we—are worth it. He went to the cross to bring unworthy people to God. Praiseworthy is the fact that God determined to bring unworthy people into eternal blessing. Thinking that Christ died because of our inherent worth or to improve our self-esteem, reveals impurity in our heart. A sincere and pure devotion to Christ sees him, not us, as everything.

A Pure Woman Hopes

Beloved, we are God's children now, and what we will be
has not yet appeared; but we know that when he appears
we shall be like him, because we shall see him as he is.
And everyone who thus hopes in him
purifies himself as he is pure.

1 JOHN 3:2–3

*B*ecoming like Jesus—that is God's overarching objective for each one of us. And although as Christians we share that objective, we usually don't want it in the pure, absolute way that the Holy Spirit is working in us to achieve. Because we aren't yet pure, we are likely to fight and resist the Spirit's transforming work. Dying to ourselves and carrying a cross is painful, and we don't like it. But God loves us enough to make sure it will get done (Rom. 8:28–30). The fight would be much less difficult—in fact, it wouldn't be a fight at all—if conformity to Christ were our greatest hope. We'd run toward it, embracing everything God allows into our lives, knowing that all he does with us is working toward that great goal.

But we don't run toward it. That's because we fear that who we are individually and personally will get lost in the process. We look in the Bible and we notice Jesus' suffering. We see that his whole life was about sacrificial love. We are thankful for that, and we love him for it, but we don't really want to be that radical ourselves. It's a scary prospect.

What's *missing* from our perspective is that Jesus endured great suffering—it was for the joy that was set before him (Heb. 12:2). The same joy is set before us. God's purpose in our suffering is always to increase our capacity for joy. For God's children, suffering is never an end in itself. Suffering is one of the God-ordained paths designed to get us to certain joys that we wouldn't find any other way. If we really knew all that awaits us at the end of suffering, we'd have the sort of hope the apostle John is writing about.

We learn from John that hope is a necessary ingredient of heart purity. Do you have the hope that John describes? Or is a current difficulty crushing your hope? You won't hope if you don't believe that God has something good to bring you through your pain. If you feel hopeless today, look past your trouble to the goodness of your Father in heaven who has blessing and joy in store for you. Consider what awaits you. Persevere through the pain; you will find hope if you do.

> For I consider that the sufferings of this present time are not worth comparing with the glory that is to be revealed to us. . . . For we know that the whole creation has been groaning together in the pains of childbirth until now. And not only the creation, but we ourselves, who have the firstfruits of the Spirit, groan inwardly as we wait eagerly for adoption as sons, the redemption of our bodies. For in this hope we were saved. Now hope that is seen is not hope. For who hopes for what he sees? But if we hope for what we do not see, we wait for it with patience. (Rom. 8:18, 22–25)

If you are troubled today, hope may seem impossible to you. Wheel-chair–bound Joni Eareckson Tada understands that sense of hopelessness. She has lived it. But a long time ago she chose to trust in God, and her hope has only deepened through the years. She recently wrote:

> Is hope *really* all that hard to come by? I don't think so. Our hope is for the Desire of the nations. Our hope is the Healer of broken hearts, the Friend of sinners, the God of all encouragement, the Father of all comfort, the Lord of all hope.[1]

---

[1] Joni Eareckson Tada, *Hope . . . the Best of Things* (Wheaton, IL: Crossway, 2008), 30.

A Pure Woman Chooses the Narrow Way

*Enter by the narrow gate. For the gate is wide and
the way is easy that leads to destruction, and those who enter
by it are many. For the gate is narrow and the way is hard
that leads to life, and those who find it are few.*

MATTHEW 7:13–14

Trying to live biblically is hard work, and sticking with it takes real commitment. Of course, we aren't left to ourselves in the battle: "His divine power has granted to us all things that pertain to life and godliness, through the knowledge of him who called us to his own glory and excellence" (2 Pet. 1:3). What makes biblical living so hard is not only the fact that we have to contend with our sin nature, but also that the world around us tries to make impurity seem good and desirable. Just look at the role models it parades before us. Today's female role models are strong-willed, independent, sexually provocative, half-starved, and surgically or chemically altered to physical perfection. But the Bible paints a very different picture of ideal womanhood. The biblical female role model is modest, godly, feminine, gentle, kind, nurturing, and known for good works. So we have a choice to make: will we mold ourselves by society's standard or by the one set out in God's Word?

We all face this choice, and we must select one path or the other, but all too often we try to walk both paths. We fear that not adopting just a bit of the world's way will make us odd, and we'll wind up at a disadvantage. The truth is that it *will* make us odd, which is why Jesus called it a "narrow way." But we have nothing to fear from it, because that narrow way leads to life. It's the broad way—the world's way—that we should fear, because it leads us away from all that is good. We don't have to conform—inwardly or outwardly—to the cultural standard, because in Christ we are given everything we need for real life.

We are all tempted to compromise, to mix in a bit of worldliness alongside our pursuit of holiness. We do want to be godly, but we also want some of the benefits that come to those who live by the world's ideals. Is this really so bad? On the surface, adapting just a teeny bit of worldliness to our otherwise biblical framework seems relatively harmless because much of what's out there isn't actually sinful per se. But it is far from harmless. Not only is compromising with worldliness dishonoring to God, it is also destructive to us. The world's promises are lies.

So what path are you walking today? Are you working harder to develop your exterior or your interior? Are you striving for your reputation or Christ's? Are you serving others or yourself? Are you investing more in God's kingdom or in your 401(k)? How we spend our time and energy reveals which path we have chosen. But how blind we can be to the truth!

A Pure Woman Is Wholehearted

And if it is evil in your eyes to serve the LORD,
choose this day whom you will serve,
whether the gods your fathers served in the region
beyond the River, or the gods of the Amorites in whose
land you dwell. But as for me and my house,
we will serve the LORD.

JOSHUA 24:15

*S*erving the Lord—evil? What on earth was Joshua talking about? We may not always feel like serving God, and when we do serve him it can be really hard sometimes. But evil? We would never say that! Not consciously anyway. But that's exactly what our hearts say whenever we choose to serve something that takes us away from God. We always choose at every moment what we think best conduces to our greatest happiness. If we believe that God and his ways will lead to happiness, we are going to choose him and his ways. But whenever we choose something else, it's because, at that moment, we don't really believe God and his ways are going to make us happy. That's what Joshua was talking about. Do you find that you cannot live without a relationship with God? To the degree that you do, you will serve him. We all serve whatever it is we think we cannot live without.

Joshua and his household were sure about whom they were going to serve—"As for me and my household, we will serve the Lord"—and his commitment is one of the best examples in Scripture of pure devotion. Joshua didn't utter these words lightly. As the one called to lead the Israelites against many obstacles into the Promised Land, his commitment had been tried and tested. But his commitment hadn't been swayed by his circumstances. How did he get like this? We long to be able to say what he said and really mean it, but so often our desire and efforts to serve God wholeheartedly get derailed by our difficulties.

Joshua's devotion was pure because it was unconditional. He was in it for better or worse. We, on the other hand, often include a provision clause in our heart contract. "Lord, I am committed to serving you with my singleness" is easy to say when we have every expectation that sooner or later God is going to bring along a husband. Would we be as quick to utter the same commitment if somehow we knew that God was never going to bring us a man? "Lord, I want to love others in your name by opening up my home and showing hospitality." But we all too often tack on to that prayer, "Just give me a nice big house to do it in." We want to show hospitality our way, on our terms. We want to serve God as a single for today, but not forever. We want to be hospitable, but not in our current environment. This is where Joshua was different. He was committed to serving God in any circumstance, under any conditions.

How was Joshua able to offer such pure devotion? He was able because of a promise God had made to him years before, a promise that time had borne out:

No man shall be able to stand before you all the days of your life. Just as I was with Moses, so I will be with you. I will not leave you or forsake you. Be strong and courageous, for you shall cause this people to inherit the land that I swore to their fathers to give them. Only be strong and very courageous, being careful to do according to all the law that Moses my servant commanded you. Do not turn from it to the right hand or to the left, that you may have good success wherever you go. This Book of the Law shall not depart from your mouth, but you shall meditate on it day and night, so that you may be careful to do according to all that is written in it. For then you will make your way prosperous, and then you will have good success. Have I not commanded you? Be strong and courageous. Do not be frightened, and do not be dismayed, for the LORD your God is with you wherever you go. (Josh. 1:5–9)

God has made the same promise to us in Christ. We can write the provision clause out of our service contract, because the Lord our God will be with us wherever we go.

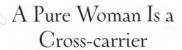

A Pure Woman Is a Cross-carrier

*Jesus told his disciples, "If anyone would come after me,
let him deny himself and take up his cross and follow me.
For whoever would save his life will lose it,
but whoever loses his life for my sake will find it."*

MATTHEW 16:24–25

*L*ife, liberty, and the pursuit of happiness" is the American dream, but only two components of that dream are biblical. The reason we find life so frustrating is that we devote ourselves exclusively to the third component— pursuing happiness—and we fall into the belief that we will find it right around the next corner. That's why we tend to be women on a perpetual quest for the next thing. We are much like the person who wrote this:

> I was a child, and it was adulthood I wanted:
> the freedom and the respect.
> I was 20, but it was 30 I wanted:
> to be mature and sophisticated.
> I was middle-aged, but it was 20 I wanted:
> the youth and the free spirit.
> I was retired, but it was middle-aged I wanted:
> The presence of mind without limitations.

My life was over,
and I never got what I wanted.[1]

To live with that mind-set is the formula for an unhappy life, because Jesus calls us to something bigger than achieving the American dream. Our purpose is not to have a happy life, and if we focus on trying to get it, we will never find it. As pastor Josh Moody recently said, our whole purpose in life is to go deeper with God in doctrine, purity, and love. He added that if we spend our energies living to look good or to make money or to shore up our reputation, we are living a wasted life.[2] A pure life is one lived for God's agenda, and that's the only thing that leads to real happiness.

How do we do this? Jesus tells us. Rather than seek our own life, we are to deny ourselves. Rather than pursue liberty, we are to take up our cross. Rather than pursue happiness, we are to follow him. But what we will find is that doing it his way doesn't lead to unhappiness. In fact, it takes us where we have really wanted to go all along. "Whoever loses his life for my sake will find it," Jesus promised.

What does this mean for you? If you are frustrated today, chances are it's because you are pursuing something you think you need but aren't getting. There are no guarantees that you will ever get it. God's Word does guarantee that if you follow Jesus, you are going to find in him the fulfillment of all you have ever wanted.

---

[1]Quoted by Charles Swindoll in Philip G. Ryken, ed., *1 Timothy*, Reformed Expository Commentary (Phillipsburg, NJ: P&R, 2007), 256.
[2]Josh Moody, sermon, "The Gospel of Grace and Peace," College Church, Wheaton, IL, April 2009.

Part Two

The Fruit of a Pure Heart

*W*e have been pondering the truth that purity is first and foremost a heart issue. Unless we begin there, our good moral behavior can't rightly be called pure; it is nothing more than a nicely polished exterior. When we have our hearts fixed on God and his Word and when Christ becomes our reason for living, we will desire much more than merely presenting a good image to the Christian community or getting the rewards that come from clean living; we will want to reflect Christ in all we do and say. That's what makes a Christian lifestyle truly pure.

Even then, however, we will have to fight for purity, because our fallen nature doesn't want to make Christ the focus. But when our primary desire is to please God, we will strive to win this battle, and we can win as we rely on the Spirit to change us. Here is how the fruit of a pure heart is grown:

> If then you have been raised with Christ, seek the things that are above, where Christ is, seated at the right hand of God. Set your minds on things that are above, not on things that are on earth. For you have died, and your life is hidden with Christ in God. When Christ who is your life appears, then you also will

appear with him in glory. Put to death therefore what is earthly
in you: sexual immorality, impurity, passion, evil desire, and
covetousness, which is idolatry. On account of these the wrath of
God is coming. In these you too once walked, when you were living in them. But now you must put them all away: anger, wrath,
malice, slander, and obscene talk from your mouth. Do not lie
to one another, seeing that you have put off the old self with its
practices and have put on the new self, which is being renewed in
knowledge after the image of its creator. (Col. 3:1–10)

Consider all the active verbs in that passage. We are to
seek kingdom priorities and set our minds on them, and we
are to put to death all that runs counter to discipleship—what
is "earthly" in us. The apostle Paul reveals here how we are
able to do this. First, we must always have in mind our true
home: we have been raised with Christ. Second, we must
have our priorities set: "Christ who is your life." Christ was
Paul's top priority, and he assumes it will be the same for all
believers. Paul said the same thing a bit differently in his letter to the Philippians: "For me to live is Christ" (1:21). The
murderous Saul became the apostle Paul because Christ was
everything to him. If Christ is our reason for living, we will
want to put away all thoughts and deeds that interfere with
that priority.

As twenty-first-century women, how can we "put to
death" and "put away" impurity? How can we reflect Christ
outwardly? We are called to wage our war for purity in a
culture where biblical femininity is no longer valued. By
today's standards, an ideal woman is independent, financially
successful, sexually alluring and open-minded, and heavily
invested in her outward appearance. This ideal is foisted
upon us in school, in the workplace, and in grocery store

checkout lines, and it has crept into the church and into our homes.

By and large, we aren't encouraged to be biblically feminine. But since biblical femininity lies at the core of a woman's purity, we must fight for it. This is, for Christian women, an integral part of how we apply Paul's directive to "put on the new self." As we do, we have the privilege of demonstrating to a scornful world how women are made uniquely in God's image, and we will know what it means to be truly free.

The greatest blessing of a pure heart is seeing God, as Jesus promised. But purity of heart has temporal blessings, as well. An undivided heart serves as a guard against temptations to sin and anxious cares. A pure heart also makes us beautiful. Jesus said that the mouth speaks what the heart is full of; in the same way, our outward appearance is a direct reflection of what holds our hearts. Appearance has to do with much more than clothing, however. It has to do with our entire demeanor. Does our appearance reflect that we are made in God's image uniquely as women? Or do we reflect the values of our culture more? The beauty that springs from a pure heart shows Christ to a watching world. There is something so attractive about a woman who wears her heart on her sleeve, if what fills her heart is love for God. A pure heart not only blesses us; it speaks to the reputation of our Savior.

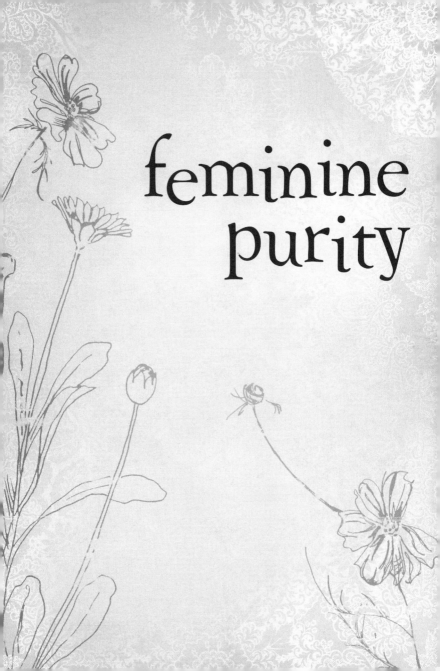

feminine purity

A Pure Woman Reflects God's Image

Charm is deceitful, and beauty is vain,
but a woman who fears the LORD is to be praised.

P R O V E R B S 3 1 : 3 0

*T*he world tells women that happiness and success lie in big breasts and white teeth, in muscle tone and trendy clothes, and today the women who have these physical assets are held out as role models for women and girls. We find a very different sort of role model in Proverbs 31. The woman we find there is the sort of woman that a wise man seeks for a wife. From her example we discover another arena for purity—reflecting how we, uniquely as women, have been made in God's image. In other words, another way to be pure is to live so that others around us see the goodness of God through our femininity. How does this biblical role model in Proverbs demonstrate this?

If you read through verses 10 to 31, one of the first things you'll discover is her priorities. She was focused on caring for her family, honoring her husband, helping the needy, and exercising her God-given talents. What we don't find is a preoccupation with personal comfort, fleshly pleasures, and outward appearance. We also see her strength. She was strong in mind, body, and character. She took initiative to get things done but not in a spirit of self-serving independence. The most important thing we discover is that she feared the Lord, which we are meant to understand as the undergirding of every other good quality she possessed.

A woman like this is a beautiful picture of biblical femininity, and it glorifies God. Are we seeking to be like her, the best sort of woman we can be? The answer depends on those we choose as role models. For a woman who desires to show that femininity glorifies God, she can find no better role model than the woman here in Proverbs, yet so many of us dislike her. She just seems so intimidating. What we need to realize is that God isn't calling us to *be* her. We can't, because she isn't real. She is the main character in the acrostic poem that makes up Proverbs 31:10–31. She is a portrait of an ideal woman with the reality of sin left out. No more will we look exactly like her than we will the air-brushed celebrities we see on magazine covers today.

We can, however, become our own unique version of her—a woman who exults in being feminine to the glory of God—in our personal set of circumstances and in our calling. Radiating biblical femininity in all we do and think and say radiates purity.

A Pure Woman Knows What to Value

From now on, let those who have wives live as though they had none, and those who mourn as though they were not mourning, and those who rejoice as though they were not rejoicing, and those who buy as though they had no goods, and those who deal with the world as though they had no dealings with it. For the present form of this world is passing away.

1 Corinthians 7:29–31

I once came across a television program called *It's Good to Be* . . . It showcased the lavish lifestyle of celebrities, and after each episode the commentator wrapped up with the tag line, "It's good to be so-and-so." Why is it good to be this particular celebrity? It's good to be Nicole Kidman because "she makes a cool $15 million per movie, owns two megamillion-dollar homes, and has her closets packed full of designer threads. And did we mention her super-yacht and her private planes?" It's good to be Cameron Diaz because "the blond bombshell is living the high life, indulging in an expensive shoe fetish, expensive, fast cars and fabulous surfing trips." It's good to be Beyoncé because "she has A-list product endorsements, a multi-platinum solo album and a rap-star boyfriend—and she takes million-dollar luxury vacations." It's good to be Mariah Carey because "where to start? How about her penthouse worth $9 million, or her 500 pairs of high heels, or even her $2,500-a-day habit of looking beautiful."[1]

What is the message conveyed by this television program? The message is that people are worthy of admiration if they are wealthy, famous, and beautiful, and if they are linked to other people who are equally wealthy, famous, and beautiful. Some decry programs like this because they shape goals and values. But they don't so much shape them as reflect them. The world apart from Christ is shallow and empty, and since that's the case, it is easy to see why women who are searching for meaning—those who are bored with life, or lonely, or just downright miserable—find such programs enjoyable.

We must admit, however, that even those of us who love the Lord and seek to live for him are not immune to the temptation to grab hold of what worldly assets we can. Obtainment of even a small piece of the world's pie holds out promise for pleasure and immediate gratification, and in our culture, it is so easy to come by! Keeping our hearts pure from the allure of the world's shallow pleasures comes only as we do what Paul told the Corinthians to do—deal with the world as though we had no dealings with it. For the present form of this world is passing away.

---

[1] *It's Good to Be . . .* , E! Entertainment Television.

A Pure Woman Knows Her Real Identity

I have been crucified with Christ.
It is no longer I who live, but Christ who lives in me.

GALATIANS 2:20

*W*hen someone at a party asks, "What do you do?" we say, "I'm raising three kids," or "I'm a homemaker," or "I'm a sales rep for Smith-Kline." We often define ourselves by what we do. But we wrap our identity around all sorts of other things besides, things tied in with the image we want to project about ourselves. "I live at 555 Elm Street," or "I attend Gospel Community Church," or "My son is finishing his residency in neurosurgery" might be the kind of criteria we use. But, as most of us would agree, none of these things is really our identity.

As women who profess faith and who love the Lord, we nod our heads in agreement with Paul's words: "I have been crucified with Christ." We say with the apostle, "It is no longer I who live but Christ who lives in me." But although we agree with Paul in theory, the chokehold that other things have on us belies a deeper reality. Our identity is all too often wrapped up in so much else besides Christ—our kids, our home, our job, our bank account, our appearance—and we don't even see it until God shows us.

Let's think about our homes for a minute. Our homes are one of the best venues for self-expression, from wall hangings to bed linens. Certainly our homes are a tremendous gift from God and often the best place from which to love others and to experience relational joy. But if we build our identity in our address, we are going to wind up frustrated because, as we well know, what goes on within the four walls is often beyond our ability to control. If the image we want to project is tied up in our house, we will fret if the doorbell rings when we haven't had a chance to clean up the after-school clutter. We will apologize to our drop-in company for the rip in the upholstery caused by an over-zealous scissors effort on the second-grade craft project. We will find ourselves tremendously anxious at the thought that we might someday lose our home. And we will refuse to entertain unless we can do it in a certain style. The truth is that our guests don't care about the perfect table setting and the five-course meal. It is we who care, not only because we love cooking five-course meals, but because we love being known for cooking them.

The only identity that brings real joy, the only pure and real and lasting identity, is the one we have in Christ. In fact, he *is* our identity—not our home, our looks, our vocation, our kids, or any of the things which, if we define ourselves by them, will only diminish who we really are. If we hold these tangible aspects of life loosely, we will be free to enjoy them.

A Pure Woman Has a Gentle and Quiet Spirit

*Let your adorning be the hidden person of the heart
with the imperishable purity of a gentle and quiet spirit,
which in God's sight is very precious.*

1 PETER 3:4

A woman with a gentle and quiet spirit epitomizes what it means to be feminine, yet in today's world where the greatest virtue a woman can possess is strong independence, womanly gentleness is viewed as a sign of weakness. An article in a popular women's magazine a few years ago quoted the author of a book about body language, on "how to look tough." Among other bits of advice, the author suggested, "Step two inches into the other person's personal space. This is a symbolic attack and will throw them [*sic*] off balance, giving you an edge." Along with the advice given in the magazine, there is a picture of a woman posed to look tough and imposing. Peter's prescription for godly womanhood is antithetical to this prescription for success.

What exactly was the apostle Peter thinking of by "gentle and quiet"? Biblical quietness certainly doesn't mean *not talking*. Nor does it mean having no opinion or the right to voice one. If that were the case, our God-given function as helper would be eliminated, since offering intuitive wisdom and insight is part of that calling. A good way to define biblical quietness is to think of it as the trait that enables us to exhibit trust in God and to rest in the circumstances in which he has called us to live. Quietness includes allowing men to take and maintain their authoritative role in marriage and within the church. It means not allowing anxiety to overtake us in the stresses of daily life. There is no need for anxious fretting when we trust that God is in control. Quietness means sitting back and allowing others to express their opinion or have their way. Feminine quietness means we don't manipulate, nag, or raise our voices to get our way.

Peter saw these qualities as a woman's adornment, as something she puts on to enhance her beauty. Isn't God amazing—to give us a means to glorify him that beautifies us in the process? The world may scorn us for it, but a gentle and quiet spirit is precious to God. And isn't that what matters most?

A Pure Woman Knows the Modesty of Personal Restraint

*Let your adorning be the hidden person of the heart
with the imperishable beauty of a gentle and quiet spirit.*

1 PETER 3:4

*M*odesty is certainly important when it comes to our clothing choices, but there's a lot more to it than merely not revealing too much skin. We are just as prone—if not more so—to overexpose what's under our skin. Revealing too much about ourselves is immodest too. When Peter painted his picture of godly womanhood, it included outward modesty—how we handle "the braiding of hair, the wearing of gold, or the putting on of clothing"—but it also included the modesty of personal restraint—"a gentle and quiet spirit," which, he said, is very precious in God's sight.

I wish Carrie had known the wisdom of Peter's words. Fresh out of college and starting her first "real" job, she came to work each day eager to be part of the team. But after just two months of work, Carrie experienced a personal crisis, and it began to affect her performance. Carrie was never at her desk. Instead, she spent the better part of the workday pouring out her struggles to her colleagues behind closed office doors. Finally, a female colleague was asked to talk to

Carrie and to put a stop to it. But Carrie didn't understand. What was wrong with being open and honest? Were office friendships forbidden? "It's not appropriate, especially with the men," she was told. "After all, how would their wives feel if they knew you were pouring your heart out to their husbands?" Carrie had no boundaries, because she lacked a "gentle and quiet spirit," the modesty of personal restraint that Peter taught. Happily, Carrie learned through the experience and went on to cultivate a godly self-restraint.

There is a time and place to open up and share our sin struggles and personal concerns, and if we are careful to apply Peter's words about the modesty of personal restraint, we will be wise not only about the time and the place, but also about the people we choose to share our hearts with. With the exception of family members, the people to whom we reveal ourselves best not be other women's husbands.

What about pastors? Most of our pastors are married; are we being immodest in taking our concerns to them? Certainly not—they are our God-given shepherds. However, there is a way to open up to them without forgoing this modesty of our person. It's one thing to seek our pastor's counsel, perhaps repeatedly. But there is a difference between a genuine need for his wisdom and our desire for his attention and involvement. Countless phone calls and endless e-mails are probably going too far. This is the point at which wise pastors will direct us elsewhere.

Modesty of our personhood is a must in the workplace. For the first time in history, women and men work side by side doing the same jobs, and they do so for the majority of their waking hours. This means that men in the workforce spend more time with their business colleagues than with their wives. Friendships naturally arise, since working together is a bonding experience. But this is all the more reason why we do well to restrain what we share about ourselves with our coworkers. The same principle applies to church committees or children's sports leagues where men and women are regularly spending time in one another's company.

"Wait a minute," we say. "We're just friends! There's nothing wrong with that." Oh, but there is. Sharing verbal intimacies with a man is the exclusive right of his wife. It takes something away from her when we focus her husband's attention onto ourselves. The best of marriages takes work, and because of that there are certainly seasons where the monotony of daily life can tempt a man (or woman) to be attracted to something or someone novel. The new and different is exciting to almost everyone, so even the most innocuous revelations about ourselves can be distracting.

And, of course, there exists the very real possibility that friendship with another woman's husband, however innocent at first, will quickly (or slowly) morph into something more. Believing in your mind that this can't happen makes the possibility of it happening even greater. "Let anyone who thinks that he stands take heed lest he fall" (1 Cor. 10:12). Our only safety lies in the humble acknowledgment that it could indeed happen in our case. We're not above it. None of us is. I doubt that many affairs begin because a husband or wife wakes up one morning and decides out of the blue to seek out an adulterous relationship. They typically develop one conversation, one shared laugh, one lunch meeting at a time.

A woman who knows the modesty of personal restraint glorifies God and lives in love.

A Pure Woman Doesn't Despise Submission

Wives, submit to your own husbands, as to the Lord.

Ephesians 5:22

$\mathcal{D}$read, anxiety, rage—there are few topics in the church today that elicit more hostility than submission. If we understood it biblically, we'd see there is nothing to fear, but a deadly combination of rebellion, sin, and warped teaching on the topic has left us suspicious of the whole concept. Sin mars everything, including how God designed men and women to live in harmony with one another.

The husband of a Christian couple I once knew used to give his wife a list of the foods she could eat so that she would stay thin, and he told her that she was biblically required to submit to him in this area. He did not understand that a husband is to exercise his God-given leadership based on what is best for his wife and her growth in holiness, not for the benefit of his ego. God designed submission in marriage for the good of the wife, just as he designed the church—all Christians—to submit to Christ for its good. In fact, a wife's submission to her husband is meant to reflect the submission of all believers to Christ.

A woman is called to submit to the authorities God places

over her—husband, pastor, elders of her church, supervisor at work, and those who make the laws of the land. But she is not called to submit to all men in general. There is no biblical warrant for that, apart from the general submission that all believers owe to one another. When biblical submission is misunderstood or misapplied, abuses of it proliferate. That, along with our natural sinful rebellion against it, leads to our dislike of it and, for some, all sorts of attempts to excise it from the teaching of Scripture.

Those who practice submission find blessing, because obedience always leads to blessing. Yet because those to whom we are called to submit are sinners, there isn't always going to be a straight path from obedience to blessing. Submission can be costly in a fallen world, which increases our struggle with it. "How could God ask me to submit to *him*," we wonder, when we feel threatened and smothered by the sin and selfishness of the one we are called to submit to. But there is no conditional submission from a biblical standpoint. Submitting is an act of obedience, even when that path looks dark. But we can trust God with all the consequences of our obedience, and we can remember that every time we obey, we are really submitting to God. Even when it's hard—especially then—he will show us that he is adequate for us. Costly obedience is worked outward from the heart. It is a fruit of feminine purity.

pure in body

A Pure Woman Offers God Her Body

*I appeal to you therefore, brothers, by the mercies of God,
to present your bodies as a living sacrifice, holy and
acceptable to God, which is your spiritual worship.
Do not be conformed to this world, but be transformed by
the renewal of your mind, that by testing you may
discern what is the will of God, what is good and
acceptable and perfect.*

Romans 12:1–2

God wants all of us—every last bit. This includes our heart, will, emotions, desires, plans, hopes, dreams, and goals. We are called to offer our body as a living sacrifice for God's use, an act that Paul calls "spiritual worship." Apart from the mouths with which we sing, we don't tend to think of our bodies as a means of worship.

How can our body be offered to God in this way? It can't, if we choose to use it to gratify ourselves. But the temptation to do just that is very powerful—every day. That's why offering our bodies to God is not a one-time decision. It *is* that, but there is also a daily battle we must wage to keep our bodies sacrificed. Because our bodies are part of this world, we are always in tune with earthly pleasures and have within us a hunger for the things of this life. That's why we find ourselves crying out with Paul, "For I do not understand my own actions. For I do not do what I want, but I do the very thing I hate" (Rom. 7:15). But the more of us God has, the purer we will become because it is through offering ourselves to God that we are remade in order to resemble our Savior more and more. Jesus was sinless, pure in every way, and when we place ourselves in his hands, he is going to make us pure too.

Although it is the Holy Spirit who performs this make-over, we aren't passive in the process. Paul gives us two action steps: we are to avoid being conformed to the world around us and we are to be transformed through the renewing of our minds. Our mind is not separate from our body; it is an organic part of it. Paul understood that, which is why he includes these two directives in this passage about offering our bodies to God.

We see again and again in Scripture that our thoughts are crucial in determining our purity. We are shaped by the things we think about. I have seen this played out in the lives of two women I know. One, Shelly, never misses an episode of *Access Hollywood* or the latest gossip round-up on the E! News network; the other, Libby, gave away her television two years ago when she became convinced that similar viewing habits were stunting her spiritual growth. Libby told me that since she stopped watching those programs, her priorities have changed. Things that used to seem absolutely necessary, like having the latest clothing trends and never going out in public without makeup, no longer matter. Today she trusts that God determines the blessings she receives, not how good she looks. Shelly, on the other hand, is constantly anxious about her physical appearance. She fears that how she looks determines her well-being, and she doesn't see the connection between that fear and the television programs she watches daily, where the dominant message is that the key to life is having the right look.

Guarding what we watch, read, and hear isn't legalism. It's just sanctified common sense. It's also obedience, as Paul makes clear. When it comes to purity, your mind matters.

A Pure Woman Redeems Her Beauty

Like a gold ring in a pig's snout
is a beautiful woman without discretion.

PROVERBS 11:22

*S*ome years ago a product was advertized by an attractive spokeswoman who smiled into the camera and said, "Don't hate me because I'm beautiful." She was making the point that there is no need to envy her because, if we use the product she was promoting, we too can be beautiful. Why is beauty something that women want—and have always wanted? The desire for it is nothing new. We want it because with it comes the power to influence. We find the truth of this in Scripture, and we find it in our culture; the proof of the link between beauty and influence is everywhere to be seen.

But beautiful women do not have happier lives than plain Janes. In fact, their lives are often much more difficult. "Cry me a river," you might be thinking. But stop to consider for a moment that a beautiful woman, like a wealthy one, attracts people just because of what she looks like. Is she valued for who she is? She may not really know for sure. And because beautiful women are often the objects of lust, they often have more exposure to sexual temptation. From a spiritual perspective, being beautiful can be more of a trial than a blessing. We see this in Scripture with Sarah, whose beauty got her into a heap of trouble (Genesis 12); we see it in the story of David and Bathsheba (1 Samuel 11); and we see it in the sad story of Tamar (2 Samuel 13).

Added to the burden is the responsibility to use beauty wisely and for the glory of God and to avoid the temptation to use it selfishly. Rachel is a woman who used her beauty to manipulate her husband and to gain advantage over her sister (Genesis 29–30). Delilah used her charms to bring down Samson for financial gain (Judges 16). But then there was Esther. She used her beauty to influence King Ahasuerus for the good of her people and saved many lives, including her own.

Did God make you beautiful? If so, it wasn't so that you might gratify yourself. He did so to glorify himself and so that you might be an influence for good. There is nothing wrong with acknowledging that beauty and influence go hand in hand. In fact, it's wise to recognize the truth of it. It's what we do with this knowledge that's key. Beauty used wisely is a fruit of purity.

A Pure Woman Values Biblical Beauty

Do not let your adorning be external—the braiding of hair and the putting on of gold jewelry, or the clothing you wear—but let your adorning be the hidden person of the heart with the imperishable beauty of a gentle and quiet spirit, which in God's sight is very precious.

1 Peter 3:3–4

*C*an we make an effort to look good and still be godly women? A lot of us just aren't sure. Some believe that putting any effort into our appearance is a waste of time and money. Others believe that it's wrong not to do all we can to maximize our appearance. Most of us fall somewhere in the middle, but still we wonder, what is the standard? What are our limits? Is it legitimate to work out five times a week? What about hair color? How about cosmetic surgery?

The fact that women—including Christian women—are asking these questions with increasing frequency is an indicator that we live in a society that values outward beauty far and above inward character. We are so heavily influenced by pop culture—by media, celebrities, and advertisements—that we fall prey, consciously or not, to the thinking that physical beauty is an essential asset. Modern technology has created the illusion that physical perfection is possible, and because we believe the lie that we have to look perfect, we live in chronic frustration, always seeking to lose just a few more pounds, afford another new outfit, and get another gym date on the calendar each week. This consumes some of us far more than we realize. Would you like to be free of the pressure?

Sometimes it seems that we just can't. It's too scary. Many of us are afraid of not keeping up in the looks department. But we can be free. It is God's will to rid us of the anxiety that keeps us stuck on ourselves. Freedom begins by looking away from the mirror and up to God. Peter said that our adornment is not to be external. Many Bible translations qualify Peter's original phrase by adding the word "merely"—"Do not let your adornment be *merely* external"—but that's not what Peter said. He didn't qualify it. Translators do that to guard against wrongly interpreting Peter's words as saying we aren't to give any thought to how we look.

Certainly God is not glorified when we let ourselves go. We are the temple of the Holy Spirit, so by keeping ourselves presentable, we are honoring God's temple. But that wasn't Peter's point here. He was talking about adornment. If our adornment isn't to be the braiding of our hair and the wearing of gold, by implication there is another kind of adornment we are to display prominently, and Peter doesn't keep us in the dark about it: "a gentle and quiet spirit," which is precious to God.

Pursuing anything that God calls "precious" bears the fruit of purity. And not only that, when we actively seek Peter's idea of adornment, we discover an abundance of delightful things. First, we find ourselves free from the pressure to keep up with the world's standards. The freedom comes as we discover more fully that God is the provider of all our needs and the source of our joy rather than what we can get by trying to measure up to the world.

Second, we uncover a beauty that far surpasses that of the most physically beautiful woman on earth. Inner beauty isn't merely a worn-out cliché. A cliché usually becomes a cliché for this reason: it's true. We've all known women who possess this gentle and quiet spirit. They may not be head-turners by the world's standards, but they are those about whom others say, "She's so attractive; there's just something about her . . . "

Third, and most importantly, we know the delight of living so as to please our Lord, and we experience more of purity's greatest blessing—seeing God.

A Pure Woman Stewards Her Body

For all that is in the world—the desires of the flesh and
the desires of the eyes and pride in possessions—is not
from the Father but is from the world.
And the world is passing away along with its desires,
but whoever does the will of God abides forever.

1 JOHN 2:16-17

A woman in quest of good looks is no longer restricted by bad genes and misaligned bone structure. Physical perfection—however temporary—can now be purchased by anyone with sufficient funds. Numerous women are emptying savings accounts into the hands of surgeons, believing that happiness is just a few stitches away. Cosmetic surgery is big business these days. Until just a few decades ago, women who wanted to be pretty made do with Maybelline products and a set of hot rollers. Lacking the remedies available now, women just a generation or two ago accepted their less-than-pure features as part of life. Today, however, all that has changed. We are living in a time when breast implants have become a standard high school graduation gift.

Although the ideals change, there is really nothing new about women seeking physical beauty. That's because the perceived payoffs for the woman who possesses it have not changed since the beginning of time—adoration, power, and autonomy. What has changed is the lengths to which women will manipulate their appearance to achieve these payoffs. Successful, happy people, we are told, are those who wear the right clothes and the size twos.

Manipulating our looks to acquire position, possessions, and people falls under what the apostle John called "all that is in the world—the desires of the flesh and the desires of the eyes and pride in possessions." Women of the world have always worshiped at the altar of physical beauty. It was as true in Bible times as it is today. We are tempted to show off and use our feminine selves for personal advantage. But from a biblical standpoint, this is antithetical to the character of a pure woman; it is "not from the Father," John said. Just before that John wrote, "Do not love the world or the things in the world. If anyone loves the world, the love of the Father is not in him" (1 John 2:15).

John also said that worldly pursuits are passing away. If we misuse our femininity for selfish gain, we are going to wind up frustrated because all worldly pursuits will eventually come to nothing, not only in eternity, but now, in our own lives.

Is the love of the Father in your heart? One way to know is how you steward your body.

A Pure Woman Bucks the Trends

Women should adorn themselves in respectable apparel, with modesty and self-control.

1 TIMOTHY 2:9

A few years ago, lace came back in vogue, and the trend is hanging on. Today's lacy look isn't about pretty trim on a skirt, sleeve, or collar. It's about camisoles and other undergarments worn as outer garments or, at least, worn to peek out provocatively. Something that once conveyed prettiness and femininity now conveys an invitation to sexuality. The trend has become so commonplace that we've grown immune to the sexuality it implies. "Camis" are worn in the workplace and even in church. "Not all lace looks sexy," you might be thinking. And you are right. But I'm not really talking about lace. I'm talking about certain trends and what they convey, however unwittingly. A pure woman is one who is less concerned about trendiness than about what a particular trend communicates about character.

Today's trends present Christian women and mothers of teen girls with a difficult challenge. Going shopping for modest clothing with a teen can be a trying experience. Sadly, many mothers have become discouraged about it all and have just given up and given in to their daughters' pleas to fit in with the crowd. But those who bear Christ's name mustn't give in, because God's reputation is at stake. It may be the style today for women and girls to walk around in lingerie, but is it really God-honoring? What is the goal? Why are women dressing like this or allowing their daughters to do so? I've heard from mothers how hard it is to find modest clothing for their teen girls. Modesty is just not a priority in retail today, but we need not settle for the sexy clothing on trendy store shelves; God will always provide what we need to adequately cover up.

Paul provided a biblical fashion statement in his first letter to Timothy, and it was no mere trend. When the Bible gives fashion direction, it becomes an instant classic. Paul wrote that godly women should wear respectable clothing, and should make their fashion choices with modesty and self-control. It's so easy today to base our choices on what's readily available and on what everyone else is wearing. After all, we think, it can't be immodest if we blend in with everyone around us. But we are kidding ourselves here. A more accurate assessment as to whether an article of clothing is God-glorifying involves both our motive for wearing it and the effect it has on the men around us. The old saying "she wears her heart on her sleeve" can be taken beyond the realm of romance to the realm of character.

A Pure Woman Crushes Idols

Every goldsmith is put to shame by his idols,
for his images are false, and there is no breath in them.
They are worthless, a work of delusion.

JEREMIAH 10:14-15

Cosmetic surgery—it's what first put the "extreme" in the now-commonplace term "extreme makeover." In order to undergo cosmetic surgery, a woman must cough up thousands of dollars, undertake the risks of general anesthesia, and experience terrible pain for weeks as a result of having her body literally disfigured—yes, disfigured, since it is altered from its natural state—in order that her face or buttocks or breasts rest an inch higher than they did before the surgery.

What other than utter vanity or petrifying fear would possess a woman to do it? As the effects of childbearing and age take their toll, some women are afraid that their husbands will trade them in for younger wives. It happens daily (even in Christian marriages, sadly), which is why more and more women undergo cosmetic surgery. Certainly there are cases in which cosmetic surgery is a blessing, such as that of a woman who loses a breast to cancer or that of woman whose face is disfigured in an accident. But the majority of surgeries aren't of this sort.

We all feel the cultural pressure to retain a youthful appearance, and there is certainly nothing sinful about seeking to look nice. But when doing so is pursued to a surgical degree, it's often a sign that our hearts are misaligned with biblical priorities. When we stop to consider both the risks and self-focus involved in surgical enhancement, the idolatrous elements wrapped up in it become evident. I once visited a hairstylist who, for her thirtieth birthday, had "treated herself" to breast implants. Pamela was quite proud of the result, but I wasn't sure why, after she told me that they didn't feel real and her husband didn't like them and that the implants would have to be replaced every ten years or so. As I listened to her, Jeremiah's words came to mind: "Every goldsmith is put to shame by his idols, for his images are false, and there is no breath in them. They are worthless, a work of delusion." Sooner or later, Pamela—and millions like her—are going to find out that Jeremiah was right: their self-enhancement was a work of delusion.

A Pure Woman Ages Gracefully

Gray hair is a crown of glory;
it is gained in a righteous life.

PROVERBS 16:31

*S*ooner or later, most of us find an increasing number of gray hairs when we look in the mirror, and when they start coming in faster than we can pluck them out, we find ourselves debating whether to color or not to color. Proverbs 16:31 tells us that graying is a rite of godly passage, but today women want to wear that crown only when it is accompanied by Social Security benefits and senior citizen discounts. So what happens when we go gray in our 30s and 40s?

Among the women I know, the majority cover their gray. Few women want to look 60 when they are 40, and reality is that gray hair ages our appearance. But so what? That's the real question. What's so bad about looking older than we are? What are we afraid of? We have been conditioned by our culture. While, biblically speaking, we certainly have liberty to wash that gray away, I think it's good to ask ourselves why we are doing it—and how much money we are spending. Many of us grab a box of Clairol at the drugstore, but many more spend $125 at the salon every eight weeks. That's upwards of $800 a year poured on top of our heads.

And then add up the hours spent sitting in the salon . . . well, it's a lot of time.

Isn't there something very wrong when we sit in the stylist's chair discussing world hunger just before we fork over $150 for her skill with the dye? "Yes," say those who color their hair at home, using a kit from the drugstore in order to save money. But is the $10 cover-up really that different from the ultra-expensive one? We all know people who spend more money on appearance than we do, and this makes us feel pretty good—until we meet a woman who spends less. That's why using extremes to determine the difference between godly effort and ungodly self-absorption isn't the answer. We actually cannot create a beauty investment standard outside of God's Word, which is what we do if we rely on extremes as our indicator.

So how should we evaluate our investment in our appearance? How can we apply God's Word to ourselves in this area? We can look up to God or out to the world before we look in the mirror. Only one of those looks will give us an accurate view of our motives. If we decide to color away the gray, are we doing it because we believe we can best glorify God in doing so? Women are going to come up with different answers to that question. Are we doing it to look attractive to our husband? If so, sitting for hours in the stylists chair can be an unselfish act of love. Seeking to establish across-the-board rules for applying the Bible's teaching about our appearance isn't the path to purity. Rather, a woman characterized by purity is one whose confidence lies in Christ, not in her appearance.

There is a special beauty that emanates from a woman who accepts the effects of aging with grace and confidence.

She isn't anxious as her hair grays or her shape changes through the years. She radiates a godly self-restraint, and as she progresses through the aging process, she sees good opportunity to practice it.

Resting in God through the changes of life radiates the purity of true faith.

sexual purity

A Pure Woman Waters Her Marriage

Drink water from your own cistern,
flowing water from your own well.
Should your springs be scattered abroad,
streams of water in the streets?
Let them be for yourself alone,
and not for strangers with you.

PROVERBS 5:15-17

*D*rink water from your own cistern," says Proverbs 5:15, "flowing water from your own well"—a common-sense metaphor for guarding against adultery. And although the instruction was written to young men, the principle applies equally to women—especially today when paths into sexual sin are so easy to tread.

"But there is no water in my marriage cistern," some complain. However, we can apply the words of Proverbs in another way. Perhaps instead of thinking of drinking as a means to gratify our own thirst—for attention, pampering, understanding—we can make the drinking something we *do* rather than something we *receive*.

First, we drink by remembering that God is the one who gave us our spouse. He handpicked him and brought about the circumstances that led to our marriage. This is the "water" we must not merely drink—we must gulp it whenever we are tempted by thoughts such as *Jane's husband hasn't been laid off twice in three years. What's wrong with my man that he can't hold his job?* or *My husband is so quiet and awkward in social situations. Why can't he be more like Sue's husband, who has that great wit?*

Second, we drink by becoming thirst-quenchers. No matter the faults our husbands display, we can offer our love, biblical insights, support, and a listening ear. It's amazing how the giving of love kills our selfish demand to receive it, and isn't this selfish demand—and the lust it produces—typically what tempts us toward adultery?

Finally, and most importantly, we imbibe water from our own cistern by drinking of Christ. He is our primary and only permanent cistern anyway. Jesus is living water. We rest in him where our husbands fall short. What we lack in our temporary marital cistern won't be found by demanding it from our spouse. Nor will it be found by looking at a different man. Jesus met up with a woman at a well in Sychar. This woman had moved from man to man in a futile attempt to find something with which to quench her thirst, but Jesus knew that she hadn't found it. So he said to her, "Whoever drinks of the water that I will give him will never be thirsty again. The water that I will give him will become in him a spring of water welling up to eternal life."

Drinking from *that* cistern is always blessed. *Becoming* a drink is too. When our marriage doesn't produce what we want, God is producing through it what he wants, and we will find ourselves blessed if we trust his ways.

A Pure Woman Wears a Beautiful Headdress

This is the will of God, your sanctification:
that you abstain from sexual immorality . . . that no one
transgress and wrong his brother in this matter,
because the Lord is an avenger in all these things,
as we told you beforehand and solemnly warned you.

1 THESSALONIANS 4:3–6

*W*hen Kathy was a child, she was sexually abused by a pastor. The abuse went on for years. Did her parents suspect what was going on? That question remains unanswered to this day. But the abusive pastor held a powerful and charismatic influence over everyone in his congregation. Needless to say, the scars of the abuse are visible still today, not only in Kathy's life but in her relationships with her parents and her husband. The pastor was eventually found out and is serving time in prison, but that doesn't undo the damage, and Kathy can't seem to get past it. Her life is characterized by anger and a deep mistrust of God. Hopefully that will change one day.

If Kathy knew the character of God, she would know that he didn't sweep aside the damage done to her just because the pastor was found guilty in court. Man's court isn't God's.

"Beloved, never avenge yourselves, but leave it to the wrath of God, for it is written, 'Vengeance is mine, I will repay, says the Lord'" (Rom. 12:19). Therefore, the wrath of God concerning that sin either fell on Christ or is yet to fall on the abuser.

If Kathy knew the character of God, she would know that God grieves deeply over what happened to her all those years ago by one who claimed to come in his name. If Kathy would turn to God, she would find the healing she so desperately needs and which God holds out to her in Christ. She would find the reality of Isaiah's prophecy:

> The Spirit of the Lord GOD is upon me,
>> because the LORD has anointed me
> to bring good news to the poor;
>> he has sent me to bind up the brokenhearted,
> to proclaim liberty to the captives,
>> and the opening of the prison to those who are bound;
> to proclaim the year of the LORD's favor,
>> and the day of vengeance of our God;
>> to comfort all who mourn;
> to grant to those who mourn in Zion—
>> to give them a beautiful headdress instead of ashes,
> the oil of gladness instead of mourning,
>> the garment of praise instead of a faint spirit;
> that they may be called oaks of righteousness,
>> the planting of the LORD, that he may be glorified. (Isa. 61:1–3)

Kathy doesn't realize that the pastor isn't really the one who stole her purity. She herself has rejected it in her refusal to forgive and let go of the past. She can't be pure while harboring bitterness. She has allowed what happened all those years ago to define her identity. Sexual abuse is a terrible thing, but although it can take away bodily purity, it can't touch the heart. Our body is really no more than temporary housing for our soul anyway. Jesus came to give Kathy and all women like her a beautiful headdress to cover the ashes of abuse. The question isn't whether it's available to them; it's whether they are willing to let go of the past and to embrace the renewal of purity that Christ offers.

A Pure Woman Masters Her Passions

For this is the will of God, your sanctification:
that you abstain from sexual immorality;
that each one of you know how to control his own body
in holiness and honor, not in the passion of lust
like the Gentiles who do not know God.

1 THESSALONIANS 4:3–5

*I*t's pretty black-and-white, isn't it? Sexual purity is God's will. We are to keep ourselves pure because we belong to God. That's what biblical sanctification means—"set apart for God." Paul tells us the way to do it is to know ourselves. Do you know how to control your body in holiness and honor? What tempts you to immorality might be different from the temptations that someone else faces. Perhaps for you, it's a particular television program. For another it might be a relationship. Whatever it is, we are called to recognize it as something that holds the potential to compromise our purity and to do whatever it takes to arm ourselves against it. It might mean disconnecting the cable service or the Internet. It might mean changing church services. It might even mean quitting our job or ending a relationship.

But we will never be willing to do so if we see sanctification as a list of rules to follow. We will do so only when we know that holiness equals happiness. God designed it that way.

Those who don't know God give free reign to their passions. They have no incentive not to. They don't know that God is a loving and kind Father who governs all things for the good of his children. They don't know it because they can't—it is known only in Christ. But those of us who do know God have great incentive to say no. The light of Scripture reveals to us the inevitable destruction that accompanies unrestrained passions. Additionally, the Holy Spirit is always at work in our hearts to incline us to choose God's ways. Therefore, if we choose immoral ways, we are fighting against the work of the Spirit within us. That's why, as someone once observed, "Unbelievers are often cheerful souls but a backsliding Christian is always miserable."

We participate in the work of the Spirit by knowing how to control our body and guard it from unruly passions. We are told this clearly by Paul, yet we so often don't, and the reason we don't is that we aren't really willing to do so. It may be that we feel we cannot, but we can. Otherwise Scripture wouldn't tell us to do it. What feels like "I can't" is really "I won't" because we don't want to go the whole way into radical holiness. Instead, we excuse our sexual fantasies and illicit flirtations and dalliances with temptation.

> "God's Word says it is better to marry than to burn with passion, but he hasn't brought me a husband, so it's not my fault."

> "My husband has no time for me, but my pastor always listens. I have to have someone to talk to, and can I help it if he's so attractive?"

"In order to take Christ to the world around me, I have to know
what's going on out there, and I can't do that if I don't understand
where people are coming from."

It is our fault and we can help it. Scripture says so. We
have no excuse. If we are serious about holiness, which is
really just another name for purity, we won't seek how far
we can go without crossing the line. Instead, we'll seek every
means possible to be as holy as we can be. Once we understand how blessed holiness is, we will want to run toward
it. Unrestrained passions bring misery; unrestrained holiness
brings more holiness—and real happiness.

A Pure Woman Is Contented with Her Marital Status

And behold, the woman meets him,
dressed as a prostitute, wily of heart.
She is loud and wayward;
her feet do not stay at home;
now in the street, now in the market,
and at every corner she lies in wait.

PROVERBS 7:10-12

*W*hen we're out and about, we often see women—young and old—who personify the immoral woman found in Proverbs 7. But a woman like this isn't found only in the dance clubs at 2 AM; she might also be found in our very own home—we might be her. Even if we do not find ourselves in this woman, there are some things we can learn from her.

It is apparent that the immoral woman in Proverbs 7 was a discontented woman. She was loud and rebellious, two traits that tend to characterize women who refuse to accept their situations and life's limitations. It is apparent that the woman in Proverbs was looking for an escape, some sort of diversion, from a life that she obviously didn't value very highly.

Are we loud and rebellious? We might be, if we are single

and we manipulate everyone and everything we can to meet a man. We might be, if we are teenagers who break curfew because we fear we'll miss out on something vital if we go home at nine o'clock. We might be, if we are married yet look for understanding, admiration, and affection from a man other than our husband. A loud and rebellious woman is one who refuses to accept the circumstances she is biblically forbidden to change and the limitations imposed by those circumstances; and if we persist in setting our hearts against God's ordering, we will find ourselves dangerously close to temptation.

The woman in Proverbs 7 had a wily heart, which is the antithesis of a pure heart, and it flourishes in the mire of discontent. A wily-hearted woman is one who will not accept the boundaries God has drawn around her life. Are we wily hearted? If so, and if we don't deal with it, sooner or later we are going to find ourselves drawn, like the woman in Proverbs 7, to secretive things done in dark places.

This woman was seen out and about on the street corners, lying in wait. What was she waiting for? If you read all of Proverbs 7, you will see that she was waiting for someone to seduce. You will also see that she had no qualms about enticing others to sin. In fact, she delighted in doing so. So how do we keep the seeds of discontentment from taking root in our heart? We do what the psalmist instructed:

> Oh, taste and see that the LORD is good!
>> Blessed is the man who takes refuge in him!
> Oh, fear the LORD, you his saints,
>> for those who fear him have no lack!
> The young lions suffer want and hunger;
>> but those who seek the LORD lack no good thing. (Ps. 34:8–10)

The seed of impurity is a discontented heart, and out it spring rebellion, darkness, relational destruction, and misery. It doesn't have to be that way, however. In Christ we have everything we need to be contented, to live in the light, and to experience relational harmony and great joy. The seed of purity is the fear of the Lord.

A Pure Woman Models Godliness

Children, obey your parents in the Lord,
for this is right. "Honor your father and mother"
(this is the first commandment with a promise),
"that it may go well with you and that you may live long
in the land." Fathers, do not provoke your children to anger,
but bring them up in the discipline and
instruction of the Lord.

EPHESIANS 6:1–4

Are we models of purity to our daughters? Are we making godly womanhood attractive to them, something they want for themselves? How they view it begins at home, and it involves much more than the clothes we wear and the TV programs we watch. It includes how we handle stressful seasons and how we relate to our husband. Everything we do reveals either a Christ-oriented heart or a self-oriented heart, and by all we do, we demonstrate to our daughters what we really believe holds value.

If we are careful to protect our hearts for Christ, we are going to be more careful of their hearts, as well. Our choice to be faithful certainly doesn't guarantee our daughters' faithfulness, but we will demonstrate to them that God's ways are always paths of peace.

Dinah, the daughter of Jacob and Leah (Genesis 34), had a stressful home life. She had twelve siblings that we know about—all brothers—and it isn't likely that she got much attention from her parents in a day and age when sons were more highly valued. But her brothers weren't the cause of the stress in her home; it was her parents. Her father, Jacob, had two wives—Dinah's mother, Leah, and Rachel—and both women were preoccupied not with the things of God but with jealousy and with competing for their husband's affection. Although Dinah came from a family of God's people, it isn't likely that she saw much of the blessedness of that in her home.

One day, "Dinah . . . went out to see the daughters of the land. And when Shechem the son of Hamor the Hivite, prince of the country, saw her, he took her and lay with her, and violated her" (Gen. 34:1–2). If you are a mother, the first thing you might ask is why was this young woman allowed to go out unsupervised—especially with those who weren't from among her own people? Our daughters, too, want to go out with their friends, and if we aren't keeping an eye on the company our girls are keeping, they are likely to fall in with some bad influences. There are many modern-day Shechems out there—young men made powerful by popularity who are all too eager to seduce girls hungry for the attention they aren't getting at home from restless, pre-occupied mothers.

Although Shechem later professed to love Dinah, she was too young to realize that real love doesn't seduce someone to sin or cajole her verbally or physically to engage in sexual activity.

What happened to Dinah happens everywhere today,

whether we label it seduction, or date rape, or being in love. The seductive woman of Proverbs 7 and the seduced girl of Genesis 34 had this in common—a wandering, discontented spirit. If we, their mothers, have impure hearts, we are endangering not only our moral well-being but that of our daughters as well.

A Pure Woman Doesn't Wander
in Her Ways

She does not ponder the path of life;
her ways wander, and she does not know it.

PROVERBS 5:6

*H*er ways wander," we are told, regarding the immoral woman of Proverbs 5, and we may find ourselves following in her footsteps if we aren't committed to God's way of making things work, his prescribed design for romance and marriage. God's design for sex is spelled out black-and-white in Scripture, and while it isn't always easy to follow, it isn't difficult to understand. If we waver in our commitment to God's design for sex only within marriage by allowing little compromises or by seeking to adapt the Word to suit our circumstances, we are flirting with wandering ways.

We may think we are committed to God's design for romance, and perhaps we are. But often we only really know for sure when our commitment is tested. Single women who know and desire God's plan for marriage—its exclusivity and intimate oneness—agree that it is good. But sometimes the only thing undergirding our support of marriage done God's way is our personal desire to have it for ourselves. What happens when we see others getting those blessings but we are left out? Do we compromise the best with what is merely permissible, or worse, what is clearly unbiblical? *God hasn't given to me what he's given to other women. He is less good to me, so I'm going to get what I want in my own way.* Oh, we don't consciously think that way, but some of our choices demonstrate our real beliefs.

On the married side of the coin, wives might find their commitment to God's ways tested if their marriage falls short of the biblical ideal. Marriage was designed by God to mirror believers' union with Christ; it is a visual picture of a spiritual reality. According to God's plan, husbands are to love their wives sacrificially and lead their families in paths of holiness. Wives, in turn, are not to withhold from their husband sex, respect, and his God-given right to lead. But because marriage is lived out by two sinners, the reality never quite measures up to the biblical idea. *God let me marry the wrong man,* we think at times, *and if God is truly good to me, why doesn't he fix my marriage? I cannot submit to my husband's leadership when he is like this! And sex? Forget about it! I just can't get in the mood.* Such a response reveals that our commitment to God's way for romance and marriage is conditional.

It's easy to commit to God's way, but do we stay committed to it if it's something we can't get for ourselves or if it doesn't pan out to be all we expected? That's the real test of the purity of our commitment to God's design for marriage. Trusting God's goodness—not only in his designs but also in how he works those designs into our individual lives—is crucial for moral purity.

A Pure Woman Humbly Acknowledges Her Weakness

Therefore let anyone who thinks that he stands take heed lest he fall.

1 CORINTHIANS 10:12

*T*he snare of sexual sin is just a compromise away. Overpowering temptation might be as near as our next bad day. So how do we avoid it?

We avoid it by learning to recognize what turns our heart in an immoral direction. For some of us, it's the desire to be wanted, to be seen as attractive. It's simply the lust to be lusted after. A tip-off is the degree to which we sexualize our appearance in order to attract men. For others, it's just plain old sexual lust, and the avoidance tactic here is simple: don't do it. Don't think about it. Don't fantasize.

Still others may be drawn into sexual sin by a strong desire to escape an inescapable daily reality, such as a lonely marriage that seems stuck in a bad place. We don't really want to give up on the marriage—we just want to escape the tension until the situation gets better. But this is precisely where we are likely to fall if we think that escaping the tension with a little flirting, a harmless cup of coffee, or a quietly shared confidence is safe because no one will know. "Come,

let us take our fill of love until morning; let us delight ourselves with love. For my husband is not at home; he has gone
on a long journey" (Prov. 7:18–20). Women in a happy marriage don't say, think, or desire what the woman said here in
Proverbs.

Women living with great frustration and feelings of hopelessness are going to be vulnerable to the idea of getting a
need met quickly and quietly in a fleeting fantasy-come-true
that they believe will never intrude into their "real" lives.
Recognizing our vulnerability—how susceptible we really
are—is the key to avoiding sexual sin. So is being convinced
before temptation hits that there is no such thing as a harmless fling. Such awareness takes humility. We don't want to
admit that we could actually have a moral failure. But we are
all capable of that, and admitting it is the first step toward
avoiding it.

That's why Paul issued the warning to take heed lest we
fall. But he didn't leave it there. He gave a promise along
with the warning: "No temptation has overtaken you that is
not common to man. God is faithful, and he will not let you
be tempted beyond your ability, but with the temptation he
will also provide the way of escape, that you may be able to
endure it" (1 Cor. 10:13).

A Pure Woman Avoids Flattery

The lips of an immoral woman drip honey,
and her mouth is smoother than oil.

PROVERBS 5:3 NKJV

There is a strong link between talk and moral purity, but we can easily overlook the link unless the words we are hearing—or saying—are blatantly sexual. Proverbs warns us about "honey speech," but words that drip honey aren't necessarily pornographic; in fact, seductive speech usually comes in disguise. Some of the most potent honey is flattery. Proverbs also refers to "the seductress who flatters with her words" (2:16 NKJV). We tend to think of flattering words as fawning compliments and buttering up someone, but if that were all, it would have very little power. It's just too obvious.

We must keep our tongues from flattering, certainly, but we must also guard ourselves from the flattery of others. Flattering words are often a hint to someone's immoral intentions, as Proverbs 5:3 makes clear. The sort of flattery that leads to immorality is dangerous and subtle, and it's something that hooks us when and where we are weak. Dangerous flattery isn't just words; it includes tone of voice, look, and intent.

How can we tell the difference between seemingly harmless compliments and those that mask an agenda? It takes wisdom—the sort that comes from basking in Scripture. "How can a young man keep his way pure? By guarding it according to your word" writes the psalmist (Ps. 119:9). A well-meaning compliment that comes our way might actually be an invitation, and if it comes to us while we are craving something we aren't getting in a legitimate way, our radar is going to tune in to the signal.

That's why the danger doesn't necessarily lie with the flatterer. Just as often it's found in the heart of the "flatteree." A middle-aged man feeling a loss of youthful vigor might be tempted to sin when he's admired by the twenty-something secretary who takes his messages. The woman whose husband is bored by marital familiarity might find herself drawn to one of her male dinner guests as he praises her delicious meal with a warm gaze and brief touch on her shoulder. Flattery—whether given or received—is an entry point for trouble. If we find ourselves exhilarated by and dwelling on a seemingly innocent exchange of pleasantries, we'd best beware.

How do we know if we are susceptible? We are at risk anytime we are living with unresolved anger, frustration, or discontentment. We are more easily tempted when we desperately want something that God hasn't given us. If we find ourselves thinking a lot about someone who has noticed us in one way or another, we do well to consider why. What are we getting from it? Why does it make us feel good?

We don't think of flattery as much of a problem, but just consider where the connection between flattery and immoral behavior is made—God's Word. Let's beware of verbal honey—ours or that of another. Pure words issue from a pure heart.

A Pure Woman Isn't Defined by Sex Appeal

Now the works of the flesh are evident:
sexual immorality, impurity, sensuality . . .

GALATIANS 5:19

*H*igh on today's list of trendy formulas for female happiness is sex appeal. Just a century ago exposed ankles were considered risqué, but once the sight of ankles became commonplace, it no longer garnered attention. Knees and cleavage came next, and on and on until today, when we see exposed bellies in the winter cold, and bare bottoms in thong bikinis at the neighborhood swim club. "It's the trend," people argue, as if our well-being depends on following what is trendy. Regardless, this is more than mere trend. There is always an underlying motive. If a young woman walks around with an exposed belly in school or in church, she is revealing a portion of her body universally associated with eroticism, and therefore, she is certainly after something, even if that something is merely an attempt to fit in with her peers. More and more women and even young girls are resorting to sex appeal to achieve something.

Using our sexuality as a way to get something we crave often carries us beyond just looking sexy. Engaging in actual sexual activity follows close behind. Some women mistakenly believe they can create a bond of love and commitment with a man by means of physical intimacy. A woman who achieves a sexy image or a reputation for giving sex may garner a lot of attention—glances, whistles, and catcalls—but such attention is no guarantee of love. In fact, it is often a guarantee of pain and rejection.

Women who deliberately exude sex appeal sooner or later discover that men typically come on to them in order to get solely what the image promises—sex. In such cases it is not love that the men are looking for. Even among those who don't know Christ, some old rules still apply, namely, that when men want love—long-term commitment, marriage, and family—they look for the "nice girl" qualities men have always sought. As decadent as our culture may be, most men still don't seek "sexy" when considering a mother for their children.

Many women don't realize until too late that cultivating a sexy image will fail to bring them the love they so desperately desire. If a man spends time with a woman because she looks great in short skirts, or because she wears a DD bra, or because she engages in physical intimacy, what guarantee does she have that he values her heart and soul? There are so many women who live under the illusion that if they can just get the guy into their lives by any means possible, then they can hook him for life. But attempting to get "happily ever after" out of sex and sex appeal usually fails. Ask just about anyone who's tried it. That is because whatever initially attracts a man to a particular woman typically becomes the foundation of their relationship. If a man is drawn to you mainly because he finds you sexy, because there is physical attraction or chemistry, you will likely discover that physical attraction must be maintained for the relationship to endure. On the other hand, if a man pursues you for your heart and soul because he values your purity and your character, your security will be much greater since he values qualities that are guaranteed to last and grow stronger as you mature in Christ.

"Sexy" is only an image. Sexual activity is a momentary pleasure. But sexual purity in a woman is highly prized by men who love the Lord, and it is prized by God himself.

pure
love

A Pure Woman Cares for the Needy

Religion that is pure and undefiled before God, the Father,
is this: to visit orphans and widows in their affliction,
and to keep oneself unstained from the world.

JAMES 1:27

Although purity is first and foremost a heart issue, the Bible gives us a multifaceted picture of this virtue. We find here in James a link between purity and how we practice our religion. In other words, do we simply talk the talk or do we simultaneously walk the walk? James was an apostle of personal application. Because we live in a how-to culture, we tend to find his epistle very appealing and easy to grasp. But when we set out to apply his instruction, we find that it's easier said than done.

Pure religion as defined by James is caring for the needy. Throughout Scripture, orphans and widows represent all the poor and needy in society, which includes everyone who by virtue of birth or circumstance lives in vulnerability. It includes the elderly, the poverty stricken, the handicapped, the sick, and the homeless. It also includes single women, children, and those without government protection. We care for the poor whenever we contribute to the deacon's fund on Communion Sunday and donate our used goods to the local homeless shelter. We care for the needy when we don't shunt our elderly relatives off to a nursing home when we have the means and a strong enough marriage to care for them in our own homes. Do we give sacrificially? I'm not talking about writing a check. I'm talking about the gifts of time, a listening ear, and an open home. Perhaps we do, and if so, we are demonstrating the love of Christ and practicing the pure religion of which James speaks.

One category of widows and orphans we often fail to provide for are the socially poor. In one of my former circles, we referred to them as EGRs—"extra grace required" types. I look back on that now and cringe. Did we think that we weren't EGRs ourselves? The very fact that Christ had to die indicates that we are all EGRs. When we used that regrettable term, we were thinking of those who make others uncomfortable by their lack of the social niceties. We had in mind those who can't talk about anything besides themselves, those who complain constantly about their problems but refuse to take the advice they so often ask for, and those who make a mess of their lives but blame it all on someone else.

We all know such people, and they are among those whom God calls needy because they are typically very lonely. Sooner or later they tend to alienate everyone around them. Perhaps we are among those who lack social graces. If so, we know what a lonely existence it is. Such people aren't in need of others' money or anything material, which is why they often aren't recognized as being among the "widows and orphans." What they need is friendship. But what they often get, if anything, is merely pity, and after a polite word or two, people are quick to move away.

Pure religion is to provide a listening ear—again. It is to

offer encouragement—again. It is to offer guidance along a godly path—again. It is to stay alongside them rather than jumping at the first chance to get away. Gritting our teeth and doing it isn't enough. The socially challenged might be unable to tell the difference between politeness and genuine caring, but God can tell.

The only way we can do it without gritted teeth is by means of God's grace. If we ask him for the ability to love an EGR, he will give it to us. After all, he has only EGRs to love.

A Pure Woman Controls Her Tongue

The tongue is a fire, a world of unrighteousness.
The tongue is set among our members,
staining the whole body, setting on fire the entire course
of life, and set on fire by hell.

JAMES 3:6

*G*ossip—it's something we don't take all that seriously. It's one of those "little" sins, something that we know is wrong but that everybody does. We spiritualize it and call it "prayer concern." But according to James, our words stain our whole body. Do we see in his description of the tongue the very antithesis of purity? How can we not, when he explains that our tongues are motivated by hell itself?

The Bible also makes a very clear connection between sinful speech and the health of our relationships. "A talebearer reveals secrets, but he who is of a faithful spirit conceals a matter" (Prov. 11:13 NKJV). Someone who gossips about a friend, a colleague, or a family member reveals an unfaithful spirit toward the relationship. No matter how strong a foundation a relationship has, gossip will bring it down. "A whisperer separates the best of friends" (Prov. 16:28 NKJV). Think about your closest friendships and all that has bonded you together—shared memories, shared confidences, and helping each other through the hard times—and then consider what Proverbs teaches: gossip has the power to wipe all that out.

"I don't talk about other people," we protest—but do we listen to talk about others? Listening to gossip is still gossip; either way we are willing participants. Gossip is a trust destroyer. Even while we listen to Sue impart some juicy news about Sally, at some level we realize that if Sue can talk to us about Sally, she can just as easily talk to Sally about us. And even as we listen to Sue, we are thinking how glad we are that we didn't tell her about that slip-up last weekend.

Gossip does nothing but stir up relational trouble. So why do we do it? "The words of a talebearer are like tasty trifles, and they go down into the inmost body" (Prov. 18:8 NKJV). We do it because it's enjoyable. We stand in the checkout line and read gossipy trash and trivia in the tabloid headlines because it makes us feel better about our own lives. "At least I don't have that trouble," we think, or "I may give in to temptation in this area but never in *that* one."

Gossip is something we are going to have to choose to avoid because it is unlikely that it will lose its appeal in this lifetime. But as our hearts grow purer in Christ, our words will reflect that. Jesus said, "Out of the abundance of the heart the mouth speaks" (Matt. 12:34).

A Pure Woman Uses Her Skills
for Others

*Train the young women to love their husbands
and children, to be self-controlled, pure, working at home,
kind, and submissive to their own husbands, that the
word of God may not be reviled.*

TITUS 2:4-5

*P*aul's instructions to Titus about godly womanhood include a directive for working at home. In fact, as we can see in his words to Titus, working at home goes hand in hand with purity. Does that mean, therefore, that business women can't be pure? Paul's words here have been the source of much controversy. Many believe that it is stepping outside of biblical bounds for a married woman to have any sort of job outside the home. In fact, until the past few decades, approval of strong business skills was given only to men—not just within the Christian community but throughout all of society. But Scripture paints a different picture. The wife in Proverbs 31—created as an illustration of what a young man should look for in a wife—performs a good bit of her work outside the home. We are told that "she seeks wool and flax" (v. 13) and that "she brings her food from afar" (v. 14). That woman also "considers a field and buys it" and "with the fruit of her hands she plants a vineyard" (v. 16). Not only does this woman work, but she does so to provide for her family and others.

However, let's be sure to note the context in which the Proverbs wife—a mother with children to raise—exercises her business skills. She exercises her skills for the greater good of others, most especially for her family. Nowhere in this passage of Proverbs do we find anything about achieving personal goals, realizing potential, or seeking personal fulfillment. We learn from her that exercising business skills and maintaining biblical purity can certainly go hand in hand. After all, she is held up in Scripture as an ideal woman!

Using our skills in a pure way depends on our reasons for putting these skills to use. Even though Paul wrote that women should work in the home, he labored alongside women such as Lydia—a businesswoman. So in order to correctly apply Paul's words, we must consider the context of his comments. Paul was referring to women who were supported by husbands and raising children. If we are being financially supported by our husband and have children to raise, yet we are considering going to work, Paul's words can serve as a siren to examine our motives. Are we seeking the good of others? Are we seeking God's glory? Will it benefit our family if we take a job? We can let such questions guide our choices.

These can be tricky questions for many of us because it is easy in our culture to confuse financial need with financial want. We tend to add much more than food and clothing to our "need" lists today, don't we? Society tells us that we are failures if we don't maximize our potential, or if we make sacrifices for the benefit of our families. But Paul wrote, "If we have food and clothing, with these we shall be content" (1 Tim. 6:8).

So as we see, purity isn't about working in the home or outside of it. It's about the motives that govern the decision.

A Pure Woman Nurtures

*Train the young women to love their husbands
and children, to be self-controlled, pure, working at home,
kind, and submissive to their own husbands, that the
word of God may not be reviled.*

TITUS 2:4–5

*G*od designed women with a nurturing instinct. We are
nurturers by nature. After the fall, God told Eve, "In pain
you shall bring forth children" (Gen. 3:16). We tend to think
of this as primarily about labor and delivery, but might it not
also include the entire process of raising children and caring
for a family? We women feel the consequences of the fall
most keenly in the relational aspects of life because we were
designed to be oriented there. A sick child, a wayward teen,
a seemingly unsolvable marital spat—we can't just compart-
mentalize such things. They tend to consume us, and we don't
let go until we have done all we can to solve our loved ones'
problems. From the time of creation, nurturing has been
hardwired into us.

In an advice column I happened across some time ago,
a new mother had written in and asked, "I'm nearing the
end of my maternity leave, and I don't think I want to leave
my baby to go back to work. Is it just hormones or should

I stay home?" Years ago, no woman would have worried that such concerns were "just hormones." She would have understood—and been encouraged to follow—her maternal instinct. However, this is what she heard back from the advice columnist: "Go back to work, at least temporarily. When you've been back a while and have settled into a new routine, you will know—not just think you know—what you want. Whatever your decision is, don't feel guilty."

Much if not most of today's feminism is anti-woman. It scorns femininity and seeks to abolish from womanhood uniquely feminine traits. The destruction of the nurturing instinct is high on the radical feminist agenda because it involves personal sacrifice. Nurturing must be offered up on the altar of a woman's right to success and fulfillment, and when it is not, it is perceived as a threat. Consider the irrational hatred toward the 2008 vice-presidential candidate Sarah Palin. Brought suddenly to the limelight, this governor of Alaska and busy mother of five—including a Down's syndrome baby—proved the feminists wrong. She proved that femininity doesn't have to be sacrificed for success. And they hated her for it.

Feminine nurture isn't just about raising children, however. Nurture is shown in kind words and in hospitality of all kinds. When we refuse to nurture in word or deed—in whatever way the situation calls for—we compromise our femininity. A truly feminine woman doesn't put her rights first. She cares for others, extends herself for the needy, feeds the hungry, and clothes the poor.

A Pure Woman Isn't Self-focused

*If you have bitter jealousy and selfish ambition
in your hearts, do not boast and be false to the truth.
This is not the wisdom that comes down from above,
but is earthly, unspiritual, demonic. For where jealousy and
selfish ambition exist, there will be disorder and every
vile practice. But the wisdom from above is first pure,
then peaceable, gentle, open to reason, full of mercy and
good fruits, impartial and sincere.*

JAMES 3:14–17

*N*arcissism—we're all guilty to one degree or another. It's part of being human. It's part of being American. Our narcissism is exposed in our obsessive thoughts about our weight. Retailers have taken our obsession straight to the bank with today's vanity sizes. Yesterday's 10 is today's 6. It's exposed in the nail salons and the tanning booths that bookend every strip mall in the country. It's exposed in our $150-every-eight-weeks hairstyles. It's exposed in how easily duped we are by the promise of expensive cellulite vanishing cream. Our self-obsession hasn't made us happier women over all. Our French tips and all-over tans have done nothing to diminish the number of anti-depressant prescriptions sliding across pharmacy counters everyday. In fact, our self-absorption has only increased the number.

Narcissism is also exposed in our claims and possessions: *my* happiness, *my* goals, *my* desires, *my* rights, *my* family, *my* schedule. Me, my, I—it's what we live for. Self-involvement breeds more self-involvement because it all just seems so normal. Think about the conversations we have around the water cooler or in the parking lot:

> "Do you think I've lost weight?"
>
> "Well, now that you mention it, you do look a bit thinner—not that you needed to lose anything. I'm the one who could stand to take off a couple pounds."
>
> "You? Don't be silly. You're still wearing a size 4, aren't you? What's the problem?"
>
> "Well, actually, I'm a size 2 now. But I've only been able to get to the gym three times a week lately, so I've been worried about my weight."

Can we imagine holding a conversation like that in front of a missionary from our church who spends fifty weeks a year in a poverty-stricken, war-torn country? For that matter, can we imagine walking up to anyone we really respect and admire and asking, "Does this outfit make me look fat?"

"Of course not!" you protest, "Those conversations are personal and private!" No, they're not. They're just stupid.

James said that selfish ambition—an undue focus on ourselves—is earthly, sensual, and demonic. This so-called wisdom does not come from God, and the results of living it out are confusion and "every vile practice." Godly wisdom is pure, then peaceable, gentle, open to reason, full of mercy and good fruits, impartial and sincere—traits that are always others-centered.

The majority of our relational troubles come as a result of living by the wrong kind of wisdom. Are you in the midst of a relational difficulty right now? If so, which sort of wisdom is dominating your heart? If you want to see the broken places healed, ask God to work in your heart the pure wisdom James describes. "And a harvest of righteousness is sown in peace by those who make peace" (v. 18).

A Pure Woman Bends for Others

By this we know love, that he laid down his life for us, and we ought to lay down our lives for the brothers.

1 JOHN 3:16

*W*hen I was a little girl, I was fascinated by Pippi Longstocking. It wasn't her unique capabilities that captivated me, or her friendliness, or her pigtails; it was the fact that she lived all by herself. There was something very appealing to me about that, even at nine years old.

Living alone can be a tremendous blessing. When upset or lonely, it is easier to turn first to God because there is no human comfort near at hand. Personally speaking, I attribute a good bit of my growth in the Christian life to the fact that I've lived alone for many years. However, there are certainly downsides. One of the downsides, especially for those who have lived alone for a long time, is getting so used to the freedom and independence of the lifestyle that we lose the willingness to bend for other people. We don't see that we've lost flexibility, however, because our *bendability* rarely gets tested!

But it's not just those who live alone who can be protective of their time, their money, and their personal space. We are all susceptible to getting set in our ways. When we find something that works for us—an exercise routine, a menu, a television show, an hour of quiet—we find discomfort in being asked to forego it.

> "Well, I could never marry that guy. We're just too different and it would make life difficult. We're just not compatible."

> "I think I'll take a pass on that short-term missions trip. I mean, do you know what the food is like in that region? Besides, I need my hypo-allergenic pillow for sleeping."

> "I really don't want to be alone for the holiday, but I'm going to decline the invitation to spend it at the Johnsons'. They eat dinner in the middle of day, and I like to have my meal in the evening."

We can all too easily mislabel our selfishness under the heading of compatibility or convenience.

The happiest families are often the largest families, those with children and pets crawling all over each other and making much noise at the dinner table. The mothers in such homes tend to be the most laid-back. They aren't easily upset by a food spill or a drop-in guest. These moms have never had an opportunity to get set in their ways, so they don't feel that they are missing out on what the rest of us so jealously guard.

Fighting to protect our most cherished hours and activities doesn't lead to happiness, but it can lead to loneliness. That's because there just isn't any love in it. Christian love in its purest form rolls with the punches.

A Pure Woman Gives Up Her Rights

What causes quarrels and what causes fights among you?
Is it not this, that your passions are at war within you?
You desire and do not have, so you murder.
You covet and cannot obtain, so you fight and quarrel.
You do not have, because you do not ask.
You ask and do not receive, because you ask wrongly,
to spend it on your passions.

JAMES 4:1-3

I have a right to that promotion."

"I have a right to expect my husband to put me ahead of everything else."

"I have a right to some peace and quiet."

"I have a right to be happy."

Do we believe that? Do we believe that we have a "right" to be happy? The Bible doesn't have much to say about personal rights. On the other hand, it has a lot to say about self death. From a biblical perspective, we really have no rights at all other than those given us through the merits of Jesus Christ.

Everything we have is pure grace. We are way too sinful to claim any sort of rights. But since God is a good, kind, loving Father, we can be sure we will always have everything we need. There's no need to clamor for more. If we don't have something we want, or think we need, or feel we have a right to, we can trust that God's way with us is best.

Here is how we can tell if we have a rights-based outlook: we are constantly on the lookout for put-downs, slights, or unfair treatment, and we are prone to read personal injury into every conflict that arises. We tend to be overly sensitive—and basically just difficult to live with. It might help us to realize that being willing to give up what we feel are our rights is less about submission to any person than it is about submission to God. In our relationship with God, submission and trust go hand in hand.

This certainly doesn't mean that we cannot make every effort to change a bad situation. In fact, God has given us the faculties to know when things are wrong so that we will seek to make things better. But knowing when something is wrong is rarely our problem. More often, our problem lies with insisting upon the outcome we want and think we need. The truth is that there are things we need that we will never get in this lifetime. But that's not because God is unable to provide them. He is able, and he does provide us with everything he knows we need. Sometimes what we need most is to have our rights violated. Here's why:

> Count it all joy, my brothers, when you meet trials of various kinds, for you know that the testing of your faith produces steadfastness. And let steadfastness have its full effect, that you may be perfect and complete, lacking in nothing. (James 1:2–4)

When God withholds, it is always to bring us to the place where we lack nothing. And he knows the best way to accomplish that.

Jesus had rights—because he was God, he had supreme rights. But he chose to lay down his rights for us. "Jesus . . . though he was in the form of God, did not count equality with God a thing to be grasped, but made himself nothing, taking the form of a servant" (Phil. 2:6–7). The very fact that Jesus laid down his rights shows us that doing so is godly. And if he, being God, was willing to do so for sinners, can we not do so for him and for one another?

Epilogue
A Pure Woman Perseveres in Purity

Therefore, since we are surrounded by so great a cloud
of witnesses, let us also lay aside every weight,
and sin which clings so closely, and let us run with
endurance the race that is set before us.

HEBREWS 12:1

*F*aith conquers. Faith is what enables us to overcome trials and pain and sin. But faith isn't a weapon in our hands. It is the link between trust and the power of God. The "cloud of witnesses" the biblical author is referring to are those who overcame tremendous obstacles, moved mountains, broke the power of sin, and stepped out against all odds (see Hebrews 11). Each one did it by faith, and if they did it, we can too. With that encouragement, the author of Hebrews tells us to lay aside everything that interferes with a whole-hearted passion for Christ.

There are two things mentioned in Hebrews 12:1 that disrupt our race. One is obvious—sin. If we have walked with the Lord for any length of time, we know that sin is a barrier to our fellowship with God and to our growth in holiness.

The other barrier is what the writer of Hebrews refers to

as "weight." We are to lay aside every weight. Such weights might be sinful things, but not necessarily. There are many legitimate pleasures and comforts that might interfere with our Christian walk. Setting these aside can prove even harder than forsaking sin because the negative impact they have can be harder to see. Such weights often don't sow seeds of destruction as readily. If something good in and of itself is having a negative effect on our spiritual life, detecting it as such can be trickier. And once we have detected it, we are more likely to try to simply tweak it a bit rather than give it up completely. The grays of the Christian life can be more perplexing and troublesome than the black-and-whites.

For some, the weight might be a particular television program. It might be watching television at all. For others it might be a hobby. Perhaps it's a relationship. Whatever it might be, if there is a hindrance, the Holy Spirit lets us know—if we are willing to know. A loss of interest in prayer and time in the Word, a loss of joy and peace, and a diminishing of fruitfulness are some of the tip-offs. The remedy is clearly spelled out for us here: "lay aside every weight." The problem is that often we don't do it. We seek a compromise instead. But if this is our approach, the issue doesn't go away and the weight doesn't lift.

If we suspect that God is putting his finger on something in our lives but we don't deal with it, we will stop going forward spiritually. In fact, we will go backward, because there is no neutrality in the Christian life. Either we are going forward or we are going backward. Some things we hang onto because we see others enjoying them, and we don't want to be deprived or left out. Or perhaps we fear being too extreme or legalistic; yet, an overly sensitive conscience is rarely our problem. And even if it is, we are instructed in Scripture not to violate our conscience.

If we sense something is wrong, the worst thing we can do is hang onto it, because what we are really doing is trying to have both God and the pleasures of this life. Sometimes, enjoying a deeper walk with God entails giving up perfectly legitimate comforts, and our willingness to do so—or not—is the test of a pure heart. Will we let go of something if we believe that it's a hindrance to our walk and our service? Or will we be content with compromise?

We end as we began—with Jesus' words: "Blessed are the pure in heart, for they shall see God." Do we want this blessing? God longs for us to have it. He wants our hearts and he wants to give us his heart. Indeed, he has already given it—through his Son, Jesus Christ our Lord. Becoming a pure woman doesn't lead to a white-washed, boring life. It leads to a life lived in undiluted joy.